Late Victorian Farce

Theater and Dramatic Studies, No. 40

Oscar G. Brockett, Series Editor

Leslie Waggener Professor of Fine Arts
and Professor of Drama
The University of Texas at Austin

Other Titles in This Series

Late Victorian Farce

by
Jeffrey H. Huberman

UMI Research
Press

Ann Arbor, Michigan

Produced and distributed by
UMI Research Press
an imprint of
University Microfilms, Inc.
Ann Arbor, Michigan 48106

Library of Congress Cataloging in Publication Data

Huberman, Jeffrey H. (Jeffrey Howard), 1948-
Late Victorian farce.

(Theater and dramatic studies ; no. 40)
Revision of the author's thesis (Ph.D.)—
Indiana University, 1979.
  Bibliography: p.
  Includes index.
  1. English drama—19th century—History and
criticism. 2. English farces—History and criticism.
3. English drama—French influences. 4. Theater—
Great Britain—History—19th century. 5. French
farces—Adaptations. 6. Farce. I. Title. II. Series.
PR734.F35H8 1986   822'.0523'09   86-16154
ISBN 0-8357-1774-7 (alk. paper)

For my sons
Jacob Jonathan Huberman
and
David Aaron Huberman

Poster for the Opening of *Charley's Aunt*, 1892
(Photograph from the Mander and Mitcheson Theatre Collection)

Contents

Figures

Acknowledgments

I am deeply indebted to many persons for their assistance and encouragement in completing this book.

I would like to thank Peter Nauman, William Whitman, Stacey Jones, Thomas Gunning, Mary Beth McAvoy, Suzanne Suessen, and Michelle Slitor for their help in securing photographs, verifying data, and proofreading copy. Mrs. Partington-Omar, curator of the Theatre Collection at the Clock Museum, Bury St. Edmunds, Suffolk and Mr. Joe Mitcheson of the Mander and Mitcheson Theatre Collection were especially helpful in locating important memorabilia on the original production of *Charley's Aunt*.

I am very grateful to my friends and colleagues, Jon Farris, D. Terry Williams, James S. Moy, Brant Pope, Charlotte Ettinger, Whitney White, Robert Hetherington, and Dietrich Snelling for their unwavering encouragement and scholarly and artistic expertise. I owe a particular debt of thanks to my mentors in the study and practice of theatre art: William Dykins, Wandalee Henshaw, Ralph Allen, Richard Scammon, Eugene Bristow, Howard Stein, and, of course, Hubert Heffner. I am especially indebted to Oscar Brockett, for his guidance and wisdom.

My wife, Raquel Beniflah Huberman, was crucial to the completion of this book. She made sure I had the time and support to adhere to a disciplined writing schedule. Her patience was, at times, heroic.

The love and unwavering devotion of my mother, Ruth Huberman, and my brother, Mark Huberman, have kept me happy, healthy, and sane from the very beginning of this project.

Above all, I would like to thank my father, Max Huberman, the most creative performer and intellectually astute writer I have ever encountered. His insight and advice on every detail of this book have been indispensable. A man of peace, he has sought to cure the problems of the world as a rebel, a poet, and most effectively as a clown.

Introduction

A dramatic author, on presenting a farce to Mr. Kemble for the then new Theatre Royal, Covent Garden, assured him that it was a good piece, and by no means to be laughed at.
— The Theatre, March 1881

Of all the dramatic forms that flourished in London in the late nineteenth century, none was more popular with the large theatre-going public than farce. Although farce had been a significant and popular part of English drama since the medieval era, the last quarter of the nineteenth century was its period of greatest popularity. Indeed, for the years 1875–1900 the Lord Chamberlain's *Daybook* lists over 1000 new plays labeled either "farce" or "farcical comedy" that were submitted for licensing for professional production in London.

While farce was very popular with London audiences throughout the 1900s,[1] there are distinct differences between those of the first three-quarters of the century and those of the latter part. From about 1800 to the mid-seventies farces were mainly short one- or two-act pieces written as afterpieces or curtain-raisers to other full-length forms such as melodramas, Shakespearean revivals, and especially sentimental comedies. But in 1875 the full-length British "farcical comedy" suddenly appeared. For the next twenty-five years these three-act plays were not only the main attraction of an evening's entertainment, they constituted the overwhelming majority of farces produced.

The early works of W. S. Gilbert, H. J. Byron, and Sidney Grundy laid the foundation for this change. Throughout the rest of the century such playwrights as C. H. Hawtrey, Arthur Wing Pinero, J. H. Darnley, and Brandon Thomas experimented with, refined, and perfected the form of full-length British farce. Their works played to some of the largest audiences ever and set new records for the long run in the British theatre. The great vogue enjoyed by farce reached its peak in the 1890s but by 1900 had almost completely disappeared—almost as suddenly as it had appeared. This study explores this dramatic phenomenon of the late nineteenth-century British theatre.

There has been little in-depth analysis of the full-length farces of the late Victorian period. Indeed, most dramatic studies simply ignore them altogether or treat them with disdain. For example, in the fifth volume of his *History of the British Drama, 1660–1900*, Allardyce Nicoll describes the farces of the period as "violently exaggerated and almost unbelievably inane" while conceding that these plays "mightily pleased the public."[2] Two of the most popular farces of the period (and perhaps of all time), Charles H. Hawtrey's *The Private Secretary* (1884) and Brandon Thomas's *Charley's Aunt* (1892), are described by Nicoll as "utterly beneath contempt."[3]

Even the major nineteenth-century critics disliked the farces that were so popular. Bernard Shaw and A. B. Walkley loudly decried the genre. William Archer, who had some good words for Pinero's farces—but only insofar as they contained elements of mannered comedy—condemned *Charley's Aunt* and the Paulton brothers' enormously successful *Niobe, All Smiles* (1890) as being of the "lower order of farce [that was guilty of] gross supersaturation."[4] In his contemporary survey of the period, *The English Stage*, P. M. Augustin Filon treats the full-length farce in a like manner: "Of inferior dramatic forms, two still survive and have even extended their clientele. Farce has called for elbow room; it takes three acts now instead of one to spread itself in."[5]

The reasons for these attitudes are several. First, the bias against the farces of the period undoubtedly is owing in large part to the general critical prejudice against Victorian drama in general. Eric Bentley best describes the modern conception of nineteenth-century playwriting:

> To the extent that the history of Victorian theatre and drama is taught at all in the schools, the word has been that before Shaw and Wilde there were only some shadowy and austere figures like Bulwer-Lytton and Tom Robertson. This is misleading because the real glory of the Victorian stage lay in the farce, the extravaganza, and the comic opera.[6]

A second and less obvious reason for the biased attitudes against the farces is that scholars of the late Victorian period have tended to limit their research to the so-called superior dramatic forms. This is essentially owing to their concern for the revolution in British drama evident in the problem plays of Pinero, Henry Arthur Jones, and Harley Granville-Barker, and in the thesis comedies of George Bernard Shaw. Thus, it becomes the critical method of such scholars to emphasize this "revolution" by discounting as worthless what had gone before. It is precisely such attitudes that enable Lynton Hudson in his book, *The London Stage 1850–1950*, to state that the English drama of the 1880s "went on slumbering."[7]

Implicit in such criticism is the traditional view that farce is an inferior form, an idea that stems from several misconceptions. First is the belief that farce is primarily theatrical in nature, because it makes extensive use of spectacle to achieve its effects—an aspect of construction that critics seem to find more difficult to deal with than plot, character, thought, or diction. A second source of disparaging views may be found in the fact that farce does not examine human psychology except on the most basic, expedient levels. In an age preoccupied with psychological analysis and socio-economic philosophies, dramas unified by character and thought prevail. On the other hand, the manipulation of plot, a prime requisite of farce, although it takes much skill, is not highly regarded as a dramatic achievement today. Third, farce is often judged by the rules, principles, and traditions of comedy; hence the clichéd criticism of a comedy that "degenerates into farce." Fourth, farce does not teach as it pleases. Or as Clayton Hamilton points out, "Farce is decidedly the most irresponsible of all types of drama."[8] Finally, farce is often viewed as a popular form of entertainment which can therefore be ignored, since it does not attain the stature of art. The critical predicament, as Joseph Wood Krutch notes, is that "throughout history... it seems that nobody except audiences have had a good word to say about farce."[9]

Overall, the inference has been that farce is lacking in literary merit but is of substantial value as entertainment. However, as Eric Bentley points out in his essay, "The Psychology of Farce": "Merit apart, it would seem psychologically necessary to attribute pleasure to the presence, not the absence of something."[10] The identification and analysis of that "something" in late Victorian farce is an objective of this study.

There are, of course, several serious and sympathetic studies of English farce, but none of these is sufficiently detailed or comprehensive in its treatment of the late nineteenth-century variety. Of full-length works, Werner Klemm's *Die Englische Farce im 19 Jahrhundert* and Leo Hughes' *A Century of English Farce*[11] are most pertinent. Klemm's work is devoted mainly to descriptions of the character types found in Victorian farce. It is valuable primarily for its historical survey of English farce from the medieval period through the nineteenth century and for its detailed bibliography. Hughes' work is relevant to the topic here mainly for its background information, since it deals exclusively and comprehensively with eighteenth-century farce.

Of essays and commentaries, the most relevant is Michael Booth's "Introduction" to his anthology of nineteenth-century English farces. Stating emphatically that "farce is not as simple and artless as it might appear,"[12] Booth provides a particularly good analysis of the mid-century one-act farces.

Thus, detailed information on the development of the full-length Victorian farces must be gleaned almost entirely from primary sources. A large number of the most significant farces were published contemporaneously with their original productions. Fortunately these editions (primarily Lacy's and French's acting editions) sought to give the reader a clear and accurate account of the plays as they appeared in performance. The detailed stage directions are invaluable for analyzing the way in which spectacle was used in these plays.

Especially useful for gauging the relative popularity and contemporary critical opinion of the farces of the period are reviews and commentaries from newspapers and periodicals. The most important newspapers in terms of theatrical coverage were *The Times, Daily Telegraph, The Illustrated London News,* and the *Dramatic Mirror.* Similarly, such magazines as *The Saturday Review, The Athenaeum, The Academy, The Spectator, The Graphic,* and *The Theatre* provided extensive theatrical coverage. Clement Scott's journal, *The Theatre,* is a particularly good source as far as farce is concerned. Despite Scott's extremely puritanical concepts of stage propriety, the reviewers for this monthly magazine were usually careful to distinguish between what they called the constructive (i.e., skill in constructing intricate plots) merits of a farce from the literary merits of other plays. Other helpful secondary sources include biographies, memoirs, histories of the period, theoretical studies, memorabilia, and similar reference materials.

The primary organization of this study is by the chronological evolution of the nature and structure of the farces. However, the problem of defining or classifying plays as farces has been complicated by the fact that farce writers have never felt obliged to justify, let alone define, what they were doing— content merely to go their happy ways creating marvelously funny plays for the public, great roles for comedians, and large profits for themselves. It was the nineteenth-century English playwrights, however, who came closest to supplying definitions, since, throughout the period, all dramatic compositions were classified by their authors into categories. Such common designations by the author as "comedietta," "extravaganza," "melodrama," "comedy," "comic-drama," "farce," "farcical comedy," and "burlesque," were printed under the play's title on all published editions of the scripts, playbills, and usually in the printed reviews.

In this study those plays that were labeled "farce" or "farcical comedy" are examined and analyzed in order to determine their organic commonality. As a corollary, certain full-length plays labeled by their authors as "comedy" are also examined in order to distinguish their structural differences from the farces.

More than six hundred full-length farces were produced in London between 1875 and 1900. This study refers directly to approximately 150 of them. These plays are divided into chronological groups that exhibit certain structural similarities in the development of the form. Fourteen of the most significant full-length farces and comedies of the period are analyzed in detail.

These include *Our Boys* by H. J. Byron, *Tom Cobb or Fortune's Toy* and *Engaged* by W. S. Gilbert, *Confusion* by Joseph Derrick, *The Snowball* by Sidney Grundy, *The Private Secretary* by C. H. Hawtrey, *The Magistrate, The Schoolmistress, Dandy Dick,* and *The Cabinet Minister* by A. W. Pinero, *Nita's First* by T. G. Warren, *Turned Up* by Mark Melford, *The Solicitor* by J. H. Darnley, and *Charley's Aunt* by Brandon Thomas.

The results of this study should be a greater, more objective understanding of the drama of the late Victorian era. It was not slumbering. In fact, the English theatrical genius for humor was reasserting itself on the stage after an absence of over 175 years.

1

The Development of a Full-Length Farce

Let no one believe that a three-act farce cannot produce art.
—Clement Scott

While the nineteenth-century British theatre probably performed more pure farces than any other in history, it by no means invented the form. Surely farce is as old as man's need for laughter itself, and as innate as what Aristotle diagnosed as man's instinctive predisposition for mimicry. In fact, the basic structural elements of late Victorian farce—from the most fundamental lessons of plotting to the expert timing of vintage business, or *lazzi**—are found in varying degree and combination in the diverse forms of drama in every age of theatre history.

In England, the farce traditions extend back to the first appearances of drama. In the Middle Ages some cycle plays and interludes were pure farce. The Renaissance saw farce or farcical elements as integral parts of practically every dramatic form—even tragedy. Such major pieces as *The Comedy of Errors, The Taming of the Shrew,* and *The Merry Wives of Windsor* are among the greatest full-length farces ever written. However, when the great dramatic traditions of the Elizabethan/Jacobean periods were officially discarded by the Commonwealth government, Restoration playwrights had to invent or—in most cases—import new kinds of drama to accommodate the tastes of the theatre-going public. The idea of a farce as an afterpiece began as a consequence of new dramatic practices in this period. It would take more than two-hundred years of performing these "small farces" before British playwrights recovered the art of creating the full-length variety.

---

* *Lazzi* is used here to describe the traditional humorous by-play of actors. It was first used in this sense in connection with the *Commedia dell'Arte* in the seventeenth century.

The Afterpiece Tradition of British Farce

The first theatrical definition of the term "farce" was published in the new edition of Blount's *Glassographia* contemporaneously with Charles the First's return to England in 1661. Along with a culinary usage meaning "to stuff" appears the following description: "A fond and dissolute *Play* or Comedy; also the Jig at the end of an Interlude, wherein some pretty knavery is acted."[1] In practice, the definition referred to dramatic pieces consisting almost wholly of loosely connected episodes of buffoonery and slapstick clowning that appealed to the tastes of the raucous, young audience that attended the theatre. While a few full-length farces of this type, such as John Lacy's *Old Troop* (1669) and Edward Ravenscroft's *The Citizen Turn'd Gentleman* (1672), proved popular, such episodic, often repetitious displays of tomfoolery were found to be best served up in smaller packages. Thus, by 1700, short farces, in one or two acts, found a popular playing place as afterpieces or curtain-raisers to regular five-act Restoration comedies, heroic tragedies, and adapted Shakespearean revivals. In the neoclassical terminology of the day, such short farces also became "regular" parts of the dramatic canon.

Perhaps the most ironic, contributing factor to the reduced form and function of post-Restoration farce is the fact that all humorous drama of a substantial, regular nature died with Restoration comedy—brought effectively to an end by the hysterical polemics of Anglican deacon Jeremy Collier at the end of the seventeenth century. In the eighteenth century, regular five-act comedy took the form of one of the most contradictory dramatic genres in history—the so-called sentimental comedy, a drama which sought to raise a smile and gladden the heart of its audience by moving them to tears—not boisterous laughter—throughout its five acts. Under such circumstances, even the relatively minor position of farce on the playbill could not obscure its particular importance as an oasis—indeed, a preserver—of English laughter in the theatre. The often ignored but undeniable fact of English dramatic history is that for most of the eighteenth and nineteenth centuries the definitive component of British comedy was sentimentality. Since sentiment rarely, if ever, appeared in Victorian farce, it became a major distinguishing factor between farce and comedy.

Eighteenth-century farces were typically two-act afterpieces with running times of forty-five to sixty minutes. Since the audiences that attended the London theatres in this period were more genteel, less raucous, and certainly less profligate than their Restoration counterparts, the form and style of the farces changed to suit their tastes in humor. The episodic buffoonery of the previous age was abandoned. The typical, favored farce plot became a simple, rather uncomplicated love intrigue in which a young suitor, aided by clever servants, gulls a parent or guardian as well as a rival to win the hand of the heroine. The main characters were invariably landed gentry, while, to the delight of the patrons of the gallery, the serving and working classes were often portrayed as having superior intelligence to their masters.

Most of the humor in these two-act farces was verbal. Instead of the sparkling wit of the previous age's comedies, the afterpieces relied on the traditional diction devices of farcical dialogue including puns, malapropisms, funny character names, stuttering, and other speech defects. By far the most popular diction device used for farcical effect was dialectical humor. Reflecting its audience, this device was used as a method of humorously distinguishing classes of characters by their usage of language, pronunciation, and vocabulary.

The only significant efforts throughout the entire century to offer a full-length farce—or any regular laughing drama for that matter—appeared in the 1770s in the works of Richard Brinsley Sheridan and Oliver Goldsmith. In attempts to recapture the laughing comic genius of the Restoration they each wrote what are usually considered today to be satirical comedies (i.e., Sheridan's *The Critic* (1779) and *School for Scandal* (1777), and Goldsmith's *The Good Natur'd Man* (1768)). They also wrote plays that may be considered full-length farces (i.e., Sheridan's *St. Patrick's Day* (1775) and Goldsmith's *She Stoops to Conquer* (1773)). Of these two, the latter was not only one of the most popular plays of its time, but has since been one of the most frequently revived plays in the English speaking repertory. Curiously, Goldsmith had virtually no contemporary imitators. By the end of the eighteenth century the two-act afterpiece farce defined the form.

There was no perceptible break in the style of writing farces at the beginning of the nineteenth century. In fact, the tradition of the Georgian two-act farce with its upper-class courtship intrigue dominated until the late 1830s. The only visible difference between eighteenth- and early nineteenth-century farce was the greater degree to which the latter depended on the use of spectacle for farcical effect. The trend toward increasingly elaborate spectacle for all genres of dramatic production actually had its beginnings in the 1790s. Such factors as enlarged theatres, the growing popularity of melodrama, and the developing interests in local color and history all contributed to a shift in emphasis to visual theatrical effects. By 1815 the ideal theatrical style was held to be that drama should be illustrated as fully as possible.

In the two-act farces written and performed in the first twenty-five years of the century much of the increased reliance on spectacle focused on the skills of the actors who performed them. The acting editions of the scripts made increasing demands for all kinds of stage trickery and *lazzi* prop business, acrobatic staging, and disguise for farcical effect.[2]

It is no coincidence, therefore, that the major farce writers of the period, who were first and foremost men of the commercial theatre, were also actors with a keen sense of theatrical effectiveness. Thomas John Dibdin and George Coleman, the younger, both acted in most of their own farces. Likewise, John T. Allingham, Robert C. Dallas, and Tom Morton, Sr. wrote farce vehicles for themselves as well as for such leading comedians as Joseph Munden, John Liston, and Robert Keeley. These men were all products of largely unchanged eighteenth-century theatrical conventions that were suited to the upper-class patrons of the legal theatres.

The 1830s, however, introduced a new generation of farceurs, most notably John Baldwin Buckstone, who were more responsive to new directions becoming evident in the British theatre and society. For the most part, these changes occurred contemporaneously with the coronation and reign of Queen Victoria beginning in 1837 and had much to do with her personal values and style of leadership. As theatrical and dramatic conventions were altered, the nature and structure of nineteenth-century farce changed with the times.

The social change of greatest consequence for Britain in the first half of the nineteenth century was demographic: in 1750 the population of London was about 750,000; by 1850 this figure had more than quadrupled to approximately three million.

The theatrical ramifications of this phenomenal increase in population can be considered both bonanza and bust. On the one hand there was a vast new potential audience eager to occupy seats in the theatres. On the other hand, the Licensing Act of 1737 had restricted the number of legal or "patent" theatres with the right to produce regular drama in London to only two: Covent Garden and Drury Lane.

This monopoly was consistently challenged, legally and artistically. As a result, from its moment of passage, the act was progressively weakened. In 1766 Samuel Foote made a partial inroad by obtaining a summer license for the Haymarket, as did Samuel Arnold with a similar permit for the Lyceum in 1812. Other entrepreneurs claimed a legal-loophole right to produce "non-regular" drama not covered by the patents.

The legal squabblings, coupled with Parliamentary inaction, produced a turn-of-the-century situation in which there were two types of theatres in London. The majors, also referred to as "monopoly," "patent," and "legitimate" theatres, included Drury Lane, Covent Garden, and the Haymarket. The minors or "illegitimate" theatres included all the others. In 1800 there were a total of ten theatres in London. By 1840 this number had grown to a rather chaotic total of twenty-two. Common law reasoning held that the majors had the rights to the traditional English repertory of five-act comedies and tragedies and to regular dramatic afterpieces, including farce.

By inference, the minors had the right to perform such things as ballet, variety acts, pantomime, melodramas, and burlesque—all supposedly musical forms with lengths other than five acts.

Unsatisfied with these restrictions, managers of the minor theatres tried every conceivable method to circumvent the common laws in order to reap some of the profits of legitimate drama. Their most effective dodge was the *burletta,* a musical/dramatic form of very ambiguous legal and artistic definition. The burletta quickly became the applied disguise for the production of legitimate drama in illegitimate theatres. In the early part of the century a burletta was generally considered to be one hundred percent a musical. By 1830 it was held to be merely a play in three acts with five songs per act. By the 1840s even the three-act requirement was ignored, and one song per act was sufficient to qualify a play as a burletta. To further circumvent the restrictions of the Licensing Act, early nineteenth-century playwrights also labeled their farces with such ersatz classifications as "interlude," "commedietta," "petite romance," and "operatic farce." As long as the law implied that afterpiece farce was the province of the major theatres, such mislabeling of farces on playbills, programs, and published editions continued to be common practice.

As the monopoly began to weaken under the pressure of more successful and vociferous challenges, the minor theatres began to attempt outright production of farces. Allardyce Nicoll's handlist for the period, which classifies plays according to their handbill labels, indicates that until 1810 all English farces were performed at either Drury Lane or Covent Garden. In 1810 one farce was produced at a minor theatre, Dibdin's *The Three and the Ace* at Sadler's Wells. From 1820 to 1829 twenty farces are listed as played at minor theatres—especially the Surrey, the Coburg, and Sadler's Wells. By the third decade of the century the defiant production of farce at the minors was common practice, although the old system of intentional mislabeling continued into the 1840s.

The competition, loophole evasions, and outright violations by the minors produced a theatrical chaos that finally prompted Parliament to pass the Theatre Regulation Act in 1843. Simply, this act abolished all of the dramatic privileges of the patent houses and thus permitted any legal theatre to perform works of any type as long as the pieces obtained an advance license from the Lord Chamberlain.

One gradual effect of the Theatre Regulation Act on the marketing of farce was the trend toward the accurate labeling of dramatic forms. Without restrictions on the types of plays produced, the need for the legal hedge of advertising a piece as a burletta no longer existed. Therefore, it is rare to find a farce or any other type of play labeled a burletta after about 1850. Among the shorter works, such labels as "comic-drama," "comedietta," and "comedy" began to define themselves by specific, structural characteristics that further distinguished them from the traditional designation of "farce."

A much more immediate consequence of the lifting of the patent restrictions was the rapid proliferation of theatres in London in order to freely accommodate the city's large and diverse population. For the first time the concept of different theatres to accommodate different segments of the population firmly took hold. The London theatres, in effect, began to specialize. In 1853 Buckstone took over the Haymarket management and for the next twenty-three years made it the primary theatre for farce and comedy. Despite such a dominance in the production of humorous drama, a farce could be seen at almost any London theatre on any given night.

These theatrical trends of growth and diversification resulted in an overwhelming demand for farce afterpieces. In the new idiom of the Industrial Revolution, "mass production" of farces became the objective of theatrical entrepreneurs and playwrights. Several artistic and commercial formulas helped them accomplish this new marketing goal.

One of the first steps toward mass production can be seen in the division of the farce offering into smaller packages. In general, the basic afterpiece farce was shortened from a two-act form that played for forty-five to sixty minutes to a comparatively brief one-act that usually lasted no more than thirty-five minutes.

The lucrative financial returns to be had clearly illustrate the commercial advantage of producing these "small farces." Between 1845 and 1875 it was not uncommon for a farce to draw more than £100 per week *after* midnight, a considerable gross for that time. (Macqueen Pope points out that Buckstone often kept the Haymarket box office open until after midnight so that customers could come in after spending the evening at another theatre, pay half-price, and see Buckstone himself in the closing farce.)[3]

The large grosses, while profitable to managers, actors, and playwrights, were usually returned only for the initial run of the afterpiece. Whereas the eighteenth-century and early-nineteenth-century two-act farces remained in the repertory and were often revived, the one-act farces were written to formula, performed, discarded, and replaced by new ones.

The popularity of these short plays was such that the mid-century years produced Britain's first truly professional and prolific farceurs. Chief among them were T. J. Williams (30 farces), J. S. Coyne (27 farces), Charles Dance, the younger (24 farces), John Oxenford (22 farces), Thomas Egerton Wilks (20 farces), and John Baldwin Buckstone (15 farces). The most prolific of these playwrights was John Maddison Morton, who turned out 91 farces between 1835 and 1871.

Figure 1.   John Baldwin Buckstone, 1875
(Illustrated London News)

As productive as these men were, their own "original" output of farces was insufficient to meet the public's demand for more and more new ones. Therefore, playwrights and managers turned to that age-old, classical marketing solution to the problem of demand exceeding supply—foreign imports. The country with the largest ready-made supply of one-act farces was France.

In his 1897 survey of English drama, the French critic P. M. Augustin Filon describes the mad British scramble to obtain any French dramatic piece that could be turned into English theatrical profit:

> The way in which the English used to imitate our pieces half a century ago resembled the hasty procedure of a band of thieves plundering a house.... From 1850 to 1880 they took everything indiscriminately translating sometimes a second and a third time the same inept vaudeville.[4]

What facilitated such wholesale appropriation was the fact that there were no legal restrictions on translation or adaptation until 1852. In that year an act of Parliament declared that any foreign author retained his copyright for five years vis-à-vis translation only; adaptation was not covered by the law. In fact, the addition of a character or the inversion of two scenes was sufficient to evade all royalties. It was not until 1875 that adaptation of a foreign work was covered under the same restrictions, and by that time the great period of the one-act farces was over.

The main object of adaptation of the British farceurs was the French *vaudeville* which was approximately similar to the one-act farce. As fast as they appeared in Paris, these *vaudevilles* were adapted to the London market by the major farce writers of the day, including Morton, Mathews, Dance, Williams, Wilks, and many lesser and less prolific farceurs. Some of the most popular afterpieces of the period were, in fact, adaptations such as Charles Mathew's *Little Toddlekins* (1852) as well as the most popular one-act afterpiece of the nineteenth century, J. M. Morton's *Box and Cox* (1847) which was adapted from the anonymous *Une chambre à deux lits.*

To the English farceurs "adaptation" meant copying the plot machinery of the *vaudevilles,* but never the subject matter of the French originals, which invariably concerned marital infidelity. To the French, the farcical possibilities of such intrigues were considered to be endlessly funny. To the British of the mid-century years, such carryings on in plays were viewed as cynical, scandalous, and patently immoral. To London's working classes Victoria stood for the domestic standards of home, hearth, and fidelity. Therefore, English adaptors invariably recast the one-act farces to deal with the homey vicissitudes of marriage and family. Especially popular were intrigues of jealousy and marital feuding and the myriad problems to be incurred from visiting relatives.[5]

The one-act farce plot machinery that the British writers did copy consisted of highly complicated intrigue patterns of multiple discoveries and reversals brought about through equivocation and other devices. This type of structure resulted in a more farcically suspenseful action than that achieved with earlier two-act efforts. The overall magnitude of the one-act farces was thus increased despite the shortened form.

The basic action of the mid-century farces is invariably the classically humorous victimization of an uncomprehending, ordinary individual by a farcically capricious universe. In this farce of the preposterous and desperate predicament, the inciting incident and resolution are brought about by coincidental, outside forces without regard to the faults, mistakes, or sins of the protagonist.[6] Such a victim is invariably a stereotypical, workaday Englishman swept up by events just beyond the reach of his control; the harder he tries to extricate himself from his ridiculous predicament, the more entangled he becomes.

The mechanics of the farce plot were determined by the brevity of the play. Within the framework of the usual thirty-five-minute playing time, the emphasis was almost entirely on the action of the intrigue: exposition was presented quickly and summarily in the form of a short speech addressed directly to the audience by the victim. The characters had to enter as immediately recognizable, general kinds of caricatures. Often, as in earlier English farces, these stereotypes were clarified by incorporating their essential aspects into the characters' names. For example, Fanny Sparks is the spunky, intrusive heroine of Morton's *Grimshaw, Bagshaw, and Bradshaw* (1851), Charlotte Doubtful is the indecisive young lady of W. H. Murray's *Diamond Cut Diamond* (1863), and Mrs. Bouncer is the double-dealing landlady of *Box and Cox* (1847).

The general environment of most one-act farces was London, where the new audience lived and worked. Thus, the general scenic effect reflected the domestic milieu of the subject matter and was rendered, not in the flat forestage conventions and painted details of the previous period, but in the new rubric of three-dimensional pictorial realism rendered in a box set. Since the overall construction of farcical intrigue involves the repeated, coincidental sudden surprise of discovery and reversal, the windows and especially the doors of an enclosed set (in contrast to the open pathways of flat wings) provided a physical and audible mechanism for allowing characters bearing complications to appear or disappear with a literal bang. In other words, the doors of a box set—from the outside, to other rooms, and to closets—served as concrete representations of suspense through which a character might burst at any moment, sending the plot off in a new, frantic direction. For this reason the room with many doors became the most traditional and identifiable aspect of scenery in nineteenth-century farce.

By calling for "commonly" or "decently furnished" rooms in their opening stage directions, mid-century farceurs were setting their victims in a milieu of overwhelming domestic materiality. In such an environment the very common objects of everyday living became the household agents of a maliciously capricious universe, thus adding directly to the victimization of the protagonist. Indeed, much of the clowning in mid-century farces involved everyday objects such as chairs, tables, tablecloths, tailors' dummies, clothes, and food, creating an environment for farcical action that was easily recognized and appreciated by the large, theatre-going public.

The farce victim's violent and invariably losing confrontation with the material world of doors, props, costumes, and human antagonists was a mainstay of mid-century one-acts. What the sixteenth-century *Commedia dell'Arte* actors called "slapstick," the British named "knockabout." Of course, the assault was more to the sensibilities, rather than to the anatomy of this workaday Victorian farce. In a sense, the afterpiece farce, itself, was a kind of quick, one-act assault on the middle-class ideals of Victorianism. But like the attack on the victim, the damage to the values of working-class Englishmen was temporary and ultimately harmless. By the closing curtain, domestic harmony was always happily restored.

The heyday of the one-act farce was in the 1840s and 1850s. By the late 1860s and early 1870s, however, theatrical and social changes began to take place that led inevitably to a redefinition of humorous dramatic forms, finally bringing the two-hundred-year tradition of British afterpiece farce to an end.

The Need for a Longer Farce

In the late 1860s Charles Kean, the popular actor-manager of the Princess's Theatre, rearranged the evening's theatrical bill in a manner crucial to the success of one-act farce. Under Kean's innovative format the featured play was accompanied only by a curtain-raiser, all other incidental entertainment including the afterpiece being eliminated.[7] At the same time this policy change increased the importance of the main attraction—the full-length play. As a result, the long-established afterpiece tradition of British farce was undone. The dramatic dilemma that confronted British playwrights was where or how to include the ever-popular farce in the new bill of fare. Their endeavors to find a solution led to a period of experiments with the form of farce. These attempts were further tempered by changing social, artistic, and marketing standards.

The first of the experimental pieces explored variations of the traditional length of the farce. Perhaps the most fascinating and short-lived of these was the development of farces so brief that they could not even be called one-act plays. For instance, Charles Smith Cheltman's *Christmas Eve* (1870) is labeled a "farcical sketch," and Sidney Grundy's first dramatic work, *A Little Change* (1872), is labeled "a Farce in One Scene." The running times of these pieces does not exceed ten minutes. Such very short farces had few imitators. Equally unsuccessful in starting a major trend was the unsuccessful attempt to revive an old Haymarket Theatre practice of replacing the main play and its afterpiece with three or four one-act farces.

Much more enduring was the increasingly popular practice of including aspects of farce or farcical devices in other full-length forms—especially comedy. Such mixed dramaturgy was certainly inevitable given British dramatic tradition. From the beginning the British had mixed farcical elements in their religious plays, Renaissance dramas, pantomimes, burlesques, and extravaganzas. Only the advent of sentimentalism tended to make farce anathema to comedy. In the late 1860s even this seemingly obvious dramaturgical separation was breached.

The most enduring efforts in this area were made by Henry James Byron, one of Britain's major literary figures of the nineteenth century. As a dramatic author Byron was well prepared to mix elements of his varied dramaturgy. By the time his first comedy with farcical elements, *Not Such a Fool as He Looks,* was produced at the Globe on October 23, 1869, he had already written over fifty burlesques, extravaganzas, melodramas, and sentimental comedies in addition to half a dozen one-act farces. By the time he died in 1884 he had written almost one hundred more and was one of England's most prolific playwrights. Despite the melodramas and sentimental comedies which he occasionally penned, Byron's primary devotion was to humor. Filon describes the obsessive manner with which Byron collected and stocked his burlesques with jokes: "Hang the subject! He thought only of the witticisms with which his burlesque should be stocked. He collected them together in notebooks which in time must have come to rival the volume of Larousse's Dictionary."[8] It is not surprising, therefore, that Byron should be among the first to successfully include that which he knew best, humor, in his dozen or so ventures into sentimental comedy.

Byron labeled *Not Such a Fool as He Looks* "An Original Eccentric Comedy in Three Acts."[9] The new term, "eccentric," was undoubtedly chosen to indicate the unusual inclusion of a reduced, but complete farcical action amidst the standard, traditional sentimental story. The play depicts an estranged and embittered couple who have hidden from their son the fact that they are his parents in order to protect him from their marital problems. The father, the cold-hearted money-lender, Mr. Murgatroyd, wants to marry his niece, the sweet Felicia Craven, to his secret son, Sir Simon Simple. She, however, loves Murgatroyd's young clerk, Frederick Gantley. Murgatroyd's wife precipitously returns in the second act disguised as the mysterious lady in black, Mrs. Merton, and complicates matters. The central activity of this

Figure 2.   H.J. Byron, 1882
(Illustrated London News)

sentimental plot is blackmail. Throughout the dialogue, references are made to the cold, hard, or good hearts of the various characters—the traditional catch-phrases of sentimental comedy. Murgatroyd's improper emotional disposition is finally resolved in Act III as he begs forgiveness from his wife:

> MURGATROYD: *(Seizing her hand passionately):* Each year of my loneliness I felt the void in my heart increase, and when that ungrateful child Felicia left me, when my spirit was completely crushed, *you* again crossed my path, you whom I had mourned as one lost to me forever—and yet you wonder that I long to clasp you in my arms that I pray you forgive my wicked folly of years back. Oh! Fanny, you cannot doom me to utter misery...Say that you forgive me—say that you forgive me—
> MRS. MERTON: I *do* dear! I do, with all my heart! *(falls into his arms)*[10]

The farcical action revolves around Mr. Murgatroyd's son, the eccentrically slow-witted Sir Simon Simple, whose very name places him with his farcical predecessors. In separate incidents Sir Simon is victimized by all around him, pushing him to the limits of his sanity. Since their toying with Simon is an unintentional by-product of their own immediate concerns, the victimization is of the traditional farcical variety: undeserved, incomprehensible, and funny. In addition, Sir Simon's encounters with his tormentors are filled with all manner of *lazzi,* including food business, disguise, knockabout, a chase through doors, and Byron's favorite burlesque device—punning.

The overall result of the admixture of effects and viewpoints is one of disunity and imbalance. The shifts from sentimentality and melodrama to farce are sudden and jarring. The intrigue is therefore awkwardly constructed; Act III seems especially anti-climactic and gratuitous. But *Not Such a Fool as He Looks* was only Byron's first effort at adding laughter-producing business and action to comedy. Byron persisted, and over the next ten years wrote more than a dozen such eccentric comedies, each showing a progressively better integration of humorous and sentimental action. At first the critics were so unfamiliar with such a mixture of forms that they commonly referred to Byron's efforts as his "peculiar comedies."[11] Only after the phenomenal success of his long-running *Our Boys* (1875) did Byron's sentimental/laughing comedies not seem so peculiar.

In the final analysis the overt inclusion of genuinely humorous actions in Victorian comedies was a crucial event in British dramatic history. At first, the very idea that the laughter of farce was appropriate to comedy seemed eccentric. The rather awkward efforts of Byron and others such as Frederick Hay (*Our Domestics,* 1867) began a trend that was more and more accepted as appropriate. By the end of the century laughter was once again the definitive element of comedy. In the late 1860s and early 1870s, however, the eccentric or farce comedies were not sufficient in and of themselves for satisfying the public's fancy for farce.

The major trend-setting experiments were in the area of longer, more technically complicated farces. Two factors facilitated this trend. First and most influential was the replacement of the alternating repertory system with the long run system. Made possible by a population that had reached three million by mid-century, the system of continuously performing a play as long as it attracted a substantial audience was popularized by Charles Kean in the 1850s. Kean ran several Shakespearean revivals for over one-hundred successive performances—an unheard-of record. The long run system greatly facilitated the production of longer, more technically complicated farces, since it permitted a profitable recovery of the substantial financial outlay needed for multiple farce settings.

Kean was also partly responsible for a second important factor that contributed to the production of longer farces—the return of fashionable audiences to the theatre. Queen Victoria revived the office of the Master of Revels in 1848 and appointed Kean to the post. She not only requested many theatrical performances at Windsor, but occasionally attended plays at the Princess's. Immediately the social status of attending the theatre was raised.

The first attempts to assimilate the changing factors into a longer, farcical form were the two-act versions of the 1860s and early 1870s. While the two-act farce had always been an integral part of British dramatic tradition, these new experimental versions differed substantially from their early nineteenth-century Georgian predecessors. First, since they were intended as main attractions, they were substantially longer than the earlier versions, usually running ninety minutes or longer. Second, they adhered to new theatrical conventions in that they were much more dependent for effect on realistic scenography. Reflecting the trend in more considerable financial outlay for scenic spectacle, the two-act farces of this period all required two completely furnished box sets—one for each act.

The most famous writer of the new two-act farces was Tom W. Robertson. Trained and influenced by Madame Vestris and discovered by H. J. Byron,[12] Robertson achieved fame mainly as a writer of socially conscious, scenically realistic, but essentially sentimental three-act comedies. His three-dimensional production style was also ideally suited to farce. Though Robertson's farces made up only fifteen percent of his total dramatic output, they remain his most enduring and consistently producible works.[13] His first three farces, written in the 1840s and 1850s, were standard one-acts. His fourth, *A Breach of Promise,* produced at the Globe in April of 1869, was typical of the experimental two-acts of the time.

As did Byron with *Not Such a Fool as He Looks,* Robertson modified the label of his work to indicate its variant form. He called *A Breach of Promise* "An Extravagant Farce in Two Acts."[14] The action is a standard courtship intrigue with a twist—it is done from the point of view of the women. The beautiful young Honor Malloy uses all of her wiley cleverness to hold her fiancé, Phillip, to his written promise to marry her. Reflecting the upwardly mobile aspirations of the *dramatis personae* of the sixties and seventies, Phillip has just inherited a small fortune and decides that he should thus switch his attentions to the wealthy socialite, Clementina Ponticopp. After the complicated farcical intrigue has run its course, Honor prevails: Phillip realizes that he has really loved her all along, and Clementina is satisfied by taking the hand of Phillip's friend, Achates. Throughout, the incidents are stuffed with almost every manner of farcical device and business, including disguise, concealment, sight gags, funny sound effects, and some especially inventive diction.

The scenic requirements are two fully-furnished box sets. Act I takes place at Honor's lodgings: "A respectably furnished garret, with sloping roof."[15] In total contrast Act II is set in Clementina's lavishly-furnished drawing room which has been decorated for a ball. Both sets are perfect environments for the consistent use of knockabout business and sight gags. Most importantly, however, the exact placement of set pieces and props demanded that there be an equally specific movement and placement of actors (i.e., blocking) within each set. In other words, Robertson's plays required a director, a position that he, himself, filled. Herein lies Robertson's lasting influence on British farce—an influence for which he was recognized in his own time. Both W. S. Gilbert, the outstanding farceur of the seventies, and Arthur Wing Pinero, the foremost farceur of the eighties, credit Robertson with originating and popularizing the art of directing. Wrote Gilbert in the 1890s: "I look upon stage management, as now understood, as having been absolutely invented by him."[16] Spectacle and action that required stage management were more integral and definitive to farce than to any other full-length Victorian dramatic form, except perhaps melodrama.

In the final analysis, however, Robertson's well-constructed farce experiment with the two-act form never really caught on with the public or theatre managers. There were others who tried to use the two-act structure— Charles Cheltman (*The Matchmaker,* 1871), for example, and Herman Charles Merivale (*Peacock's Holiday,* 1874)—but their efforts were equally unsuccessful. Still, social, theatrical, and economic factors of the period all called for a longer farce.

The Farcical Comedy

It was, in fact, Robertson himself who popularized the proper length for full-length plays of the Victorian period. His three-act "cup and saucer" sentimental comedies were produced by the Bancrofts at the Prince of Wales Theatre in the late 1860s. Owing largely to the enormous success of *Society*

(1865), *Ours* (1866), *Caste* (1867), *Play* (1868), and *School* (1869), the three-act form became standard for all full-length plays by the mid-seventies. An article appearing in the December 1878 issue of *The Theatre* ascribes the three-act form as particular to English tastes:

> Plays in five acts are assuredly not popular in London, least of all are they popular at Mrs. Bancroft's theatre, where three acts of Robertson have been accepted as correct in form. This question about the length of an entertainment seems trifling; in reality it is serious. In France no audience objects to being kept in the theatre until midnight.[17]

The problem for the label-conscious English playwrights was what, exactly, to call their three-act farces. The French referred to them simply as "*comédies*" or "*comédies-vaudevilles.*" Perhaps drawing from a translation of the latter French term, British playwrights and publishers settled finally on the use of "farcical comedy" to describe the full-length version of the one-acts that were adapted to new theatrical and dramatic conventions. The term "farce" remained the designation of the one-act curtain-raiser. While later in the century "farcical comedy" and "farce" became virtually synonymous, the early use of the former term seemed to imply a slightly more sophisticated tone and structure than the latter, as indicated in the following review of George Sim's *The Gay City* (1881):

> Mr. Sims, indeed, would probably say that the writing is quite good enough for a farce, and to a certain extent, I suppose, that would be incontrovertible. Yet with a little more care in construction, a little more painstaking with character, and a little more freshness and polish in the talk, "The Gay City" might at least have made good its right to the name of "farcical comedy," and it seems a pity that the requisite attention was not paid to it.[18]

Despite the somewhat contradictory nature of the "farcical comedy" designation, the term was faithfully and consistently applied to all of the full-length farces written and produced from 1875 to 1885.

The First Farcical Comedy

The first successfully produced, full-length English farce appeared rather suddenly at the St. James Theatre on April 24, 1875. W. S. Gilbert's "entirely original," three-act play, *Tom Cobb, or Fortune's Toy,* was nearly as unheralded in its time as it is in ours. The play, however, stands as the first attempt by an English writer to fashion an afterpiece form into a main attraction. The product was so unheard-of that Gilbert used the new label "farcical comedy" to advertise his work. In the nineteenth century the idea of a full-length farce was practically a contradiction in terms.

Several major critics of the period, however, maintain that the first full-length farce would have to be H. J. Byron's *Our Boys,* which opened four months earlier. Opening on January 1, 1875, at the Strand; it did not close until four years, three months, and 1300 performances later, making it the longest running British play up to that time. John Russell Taylor, among others, refers to *Our Boys* as a farce without further explanation.[19] While the question of which of the two plays was the first farcical comedy is of negligible worth, it is important to show that Byron's play has little connection to British farce tradition.

First of all, Byron was correct in labeling *Our Boys* "An Original Modern Comedy," since it is actually one of his "peculiar" comedies in the manner of *Not Such a Fool as He Looks.* By 1875 the public was sufficiently familiar with Byron's combining of a standard sentimental comedy with loosely integrated aspects of farce or farcical devices, so that what was eccentric in 1868 was modern by 1875.

Even though *Our Boys* follows an intrigue structure, the resulting plot is not the tightly organized and highly complicated action of farce. Most significantly, the inciting incident and resolution are not those of farce, brought about by coincidental or capricious universal forces that have no regard for the faults, mistakes, or sins of the protagonist. Instead, all of the major action of *Our Boys* is forwarded by the sentimental causality of characters listening to—or failing to listen to—their hearts.[20] The play concerns the predicament of two fathers, Sir Geoffrey Champneys, an upper-class county magnate, and Perkin Middlewick, an entirely middle-class retired butterman. Each attempts to prove to the other that his method of child rearing is best. Champneys demands strict, unquestioning obedience, while Middlewick is permissive. Ultimately they only succeed in seriously alienating their respective college-educated sons when they refuse to approve their sons' prospective marriage partners. The reason for their intransigent disapproval is that each son wants to marry a girl not of his social status. Charlie Middlewick is in love with Champneys' heiress niece, Violet, while Talbot Champneys wants to marry Violet's poor cousin, Mary. In each case, the fathers have only themselves to blame for the predicament. They are victims of their own prejudice, vanity, and obstinacy. They are in no way victims of farcical circumstance. The characters, therefore, belong to the comic tradition, since they are differentiated mainly by moral qualities. In contrast, the expedient desperation of farce characters completely overpowers any ethical traits they may have.

Until the end of the play there is almost no desperation evident in the thought of any of the characters. Actually, the pace throughout is leisurely. Beginning with an early point of attack, the overall impression is one of

Figure 3. Act I Curtain Scene from the Original Production of H.J. Byron's *Our Boys*, 1875
(Illustrated Sporting and Dramatic News)

increasing despair. In addition to the heartfelt sentiment, the characters experience the kind of distressful emotions that have always been outside the farcical tradition.

The diction consists mainly of logical prose which derives some humor from actual wit, rather than the nonsense language of farce. The wit, however, is of an unrefined nature, owing in part to the fact that it was new to the comedy of the time and also to Byron's preference for the diction devices of burlesque and farce, especially punning. An example of Byronic wit is Mary's opinion about mannered behavior: "If one's always to do what's proper and current, life might as well be all rice pudding and toast and water. I hate them both, they're so dreadfully wholesome."[21] Despite its basically unsophisticated nature, it was this type of wit that captured the attention of the audience—even to the point of obscuring the overall sentimentality. The critic for the *Illustrated Sporting and Dramatic News* wrote of the original production:

> The excessive humor of the dialogue over-powers all critical considerations of the improbabilities of the characters and principal incidents...Those who go to the theatre for real enjoyment, to have a good laugh and revel in the witticisms poured forth without a stint at every instant, cannot possibly do better than occupy places at this theatre during the performance of *Our Boys*.[22]

While there is certainly humor in the diction, it is hard to find any evidence of knockabout or physical business, except for some rather unfunny hiding in closets by the fathers in Act III.

In summary, the major structural aspects of *Our Boys* are the criteria of traditional British comedy, both tearful and laughing. *Our Boys* does not deserve distinction as a full-length farce. There are great differences in form and viewpoint between this play about Charlie's father and the one about Charley's aunt. *Our Boys* does deserve, however, recognition beyond its record-breaking run. First, it proved to be a pinnacle play of British sentimental comedy. At the same time, *Our Boys* was the turning point in redefining the genre, since it was applauded as much, if not more, for its humor as it was for its sentiments. After one thousand performances *The Theatre* noted the new popularity of laughter-producing action in comedy: "In most of his [Byron's] comedies an element of rather broad farce is introduced. Formerly the two things would have been incongruous, but the public taste in this respect has undergone a change."[23]

Byron tried to follow the phenomenal success of *Our Boys* with a companion piece titled *The Girls* (1879). This play was not nearly as successful in production, probably because it contained a much stronger moral/sentimental tone than its predecessor. It was just not as funny.

Other playwrights of the period who followed the example of *Our Boys* included F. C. Burnand, whose *Our Club* (1878) and *Ourselves* (1880) proved extremely popular; Sidney Grundy, who achieved success with *Mammon* (1880) and *In Honour Bound* (1881); and George Sims, whose most successful comedy was *The Halfway House* (1881). All of these men were accomplished farceurs; they knew exactly what they were adding to their comedies.

That the humorous trend in comedy had taken hold by the 1880s is illustrated by the critical reaction to Brandon Thomas's first play, the heavily sentimental *Comrades,* produced in 1883. While praising the young author's dramatic talents, the reviewers criticized the play for being too serious to be labeled as a comedy.[24] Such opinions undoubtedly owed as much to the progressive inclusion of humor in comedy as to the phenomenal popularity of the new farcical comedies—of which Gilbert's *Tom Cobb* was the first.

The author of *Tom Cobb,* William Schwenck Gilbert, was born in 1836 but did not start his playwriting career until 1866 at the urging of T. W. Robertson. His first work was a commissioned Christmas burlesque titled *Ruy Blas.* By the time *Tom Cobb* opened at the St. James Theatre in 1875 Gilbert had written over thirty-five theatrical works, including sentimental comedies, burlesques, extravaganzas, and at least four one-act farces. By reputation, his name is almost always associated with that of Arthur Sullivan, who wrote the music to Gilbert's libretti for their famous Savoy operas. In addition to the singular distinction of his operatic achievements, Gilbert deserves recognition for his accomplishments with the full-length farce. Not only did Gilbert popularize French farce with his translation of *An Italian Straw Hat* in 1873 and his adaptation of *Le Reveillon* as *On Bail* in 1877, he was also the first British dramatist to try writing an original, native farcical comedy.

Tom Cobb, or Fortune's Toy was advertised and published as "An Entirely Original Farcical Comedy in Three Acts."[25] While it basically adheres to an intrigue structure, there is much about its nature and attitude that was distinctively native for its time and uniquely Gilbertian. Surely no one took the victimizing farce universe more seriously. Throughout all of his farces and many of his other works, a cold cynicism pervades the illogic of human behavior.

True to the farcical ideal, *Tom Cobb* achieves its effects through laughter. It is, however, a cold laughter that borders closer on the cynical than had the humor of any British playwright since Ben Jonson. Gilbert's particular methodology for achieving such unsympathetic humor came to be known as "topseyturveydom." Structurally, it was the mid-century British farceur's standard inversion of Victorian morals, manners, and sayings—but with a vengeance. The word itself derives from an 1874 Gilbert extravaganza titled *Topsey Turveydom,* in which everything is inverted, so that beauty becomes ugliness, vice becomes virtue, and the ostensible truth is a pack of lies. In one way or another, topseyturveydom pervades all the structural levels of *Tom Cobb.*

That the play is set squarely in the victimizing farcical universe is evident in the subtitle, "Fortune's Toy." Fortune, here, has double meaning. Not only is Tom Cobb a quintessential innocent farce victim, but he is also thrown into his desperate predicament by the ups and downs of his financial status. However, despite the accurate indication of farcical probabilities in the title, the overall action of Tom's intrigue is structured rather crudely. Significantly, Gilbert used an early point of attack, an inefficient form of plotting for a farce. The play takes place over the course of six months and tells virtually the whole story of Tom Cobb.

Tom Cobb is a well-intentioned, innocent young man whom luck has forsaken. In the opening line of the play he declares his near resignation:

> TOM: But everything always did go wrong with me, even before I was born, for I was always expected to be a girl, and turned out something quite different, and no fault of mine, I'm sure! *(producing pistol)* Oh, if I was only quite, quite sure I knew how to load it, I'd blow my brains out this minute, I would upon my word and honor![26]

Having recently become engaged to Matilda and recently graduated as a surgeon, Tom has borrowed £250 to set up his medical practice. His problems begin when, instead, he trustingly lends the money to his prospective father-in-law, the unscrupulous Colonel O'Fipp, who announces that since Tom is penniless, he has promised his daughter's hand to someone else. O'Fipp has the eccentrically greedy habit of promising his daughter's hand to anyone who will lend him money. Tom's problems multiply rapidly as he is led on a wild adventure by utterly ruthless characters.

Tom quickly discovers that he must compete for Matilda's hand with his conniving ex-roommate, Whipple, who nefariously offers Tom a way to avoid his debts by taking on the identity of one of Whipple's recently deceased patients, an old man he capricioulsy named "Tom Cobb." In Act I, Gilbert also introduces Caroline Effingham, an overly self-conscious romantic, who arrives to tell Matilda of her soulful, unrequited love for a suitor she has never seen, but who agreed by letter to marry her, and whom she is now suing for breech of promise.[27] After explaining her predicament, Caroline leaves. (Gilbert, rather awkwardly, does not reveal her significance to the plot until the end of the next act.) In any event the first act ends precipitously as Whipple excitedly arrives with the news that when "Old Tom" died, he left a great fortune in gold buried under his fireplace. O'Fipp immediately threatens to reveal Tom's faked death and declares himself to be Tom's only "heir."

Act II takes place three months later in O'Fipp's formerly shabby house, now richly furnished. Tom's predicament, however, continues to worsen. A

£50 reward has been issued for word of his whereabouts. As Tom sinks deeper into confusion and desperation, O'Fipp suggests that he take on the identity of yet another recently deceased man, one Major-General Fitzpatrick. Tom dazedly agrees. When Caroline Effingham and her self-consciously romantic parents arrive Tom is introduced to them as Fitzpatrick. At this point, Caroline's unexplained appearance in Act I becomes clear. The real, but recently deceased Fitzpatrick, by way of farcical coincidence, was her sight-unseen fiancé. Plunged into another identity crisis and threatened with another law suit, Tom confusedly admits that he is Fitzpatrick and agrees to marry Caroline.

Act III takes place yet another three months later in the shabby drawing room of the Effingham's house. Tom has been living under their influence and has taken to trying to adopt their romantic posturing. His fortunes take another turn for the worse when he learns that O'Fipp has cut off his meager allowance. Utterly desperate, Tom finally resolves to give up and turn himself in. At the lowest level of his sinking fortunes, Tom is finally saved in a resolution that turns on a double discovery and a reversal. Caroline's brother, Bullstrode, turns out to be a clerk at the law office offering the reward for Tom. Rather than seeking him for debt collection, they merely wanted to inform him that "Old Tom Cobb" actually was his grandfather. Tom, as his only true heir, is entitled to O'Fipp's property as well as an additional £12,000. The intrigue ends on a suitably topsey-turvey note as Tom rejects the insincere overtures of the O'Fipps for the empty romantic posturing of Caroline Effingham by accepting her hand in marriage.

On the whole, the cause-and-effect relationship of the incidents in *Tom Cobb* are crudely constructed. The magnitude of the victimization is therefore reduced by virtue of not only its early point of attack but also by the relatively few major plot complications that occur within its three-act structure. There are only ten: four in Act I and three each in Acts II and III. As a result, the potential humor to be derived from the progression of the intrigue is diminished.

Gilbert compensated for this loss by increasing the humor to be derived from the eccentricities of the characters—a traditional but somewhat uncommon trade-off in the history of British farce. Rather than the flat stereotypes typical of afterpiece farce, the space of the three-act form provides more opportunity for individualized and particularly interesting habitual traits. In the distinctly Gilbertian mode, all of the character eccentricities in *Tom Cobb* derive from his essentially cynical viewpoint. William Archer, distinguished advocate of the problem plays of the nineties and unfailing critic of all previous nineteenth-century British drama, had a surprisingly good word to say about Gilbert on the subject of his farce characters: "[Gilbert's] farces were original and clever... in which the fun arose, for the most part, from the self-confessed egoism and meanness of the characters."[28] In the

Figure 4.   Scene from the Original Production of W.S. Gilbert's
Tom Cobb, or Fortune's Toy, 1875
(Illustrated Sporting and Dramatic News)

category of extreme self-conceit are the pretentious, posturing Effinghams, described under the *dramatis personae* as "Members of a Romantic Family." As for pure greed and meanness, the O'Fipps and Whipple qualify as habitual eccentrics. That is, each is characterized by inherent negative traits. The Colonel promises his daughter's hand to anyone who will lend him money, and Whipple is a confirmed cheater.

In the course of his developing predicament, Tom goes through a traditional progression of desperate thinking that invariably plagued the victims of British farce. The first step is the expedient acceptance under pressure of Whipple's idea of changing identities with a dead man:

> WHIPPLE: Worth thinking of? It's worth jumping at without stopping to think at all.
> TOM: I believe you're right. *(After a pause)* I'll do it! (I-9)

After the initial complications, Tom reaches the next step by recognizing the absurdly farcical nature of his predicament. In this case, Gilbert was able to turn the whole play topsey-turvey back on itself by having Tom observe: "Everyone is talking about it; a Christmas annual has been published, 'How We found Tom Cobb,' and a farce called 'Tom Cobb Found at Last,' is playing at a principal theatre!" (III-27). As his predicament becomes hopelessly confused, Tom reaches the third and most definitive level of British farce thought—the doubting of his own sanity, or in this case, the doubting of his very identity. Thus to Caroline he cries:

> TOM: *(Looking at the writ):* Breach of promise! *(wildly)*...You say I'm engaged to you. I daresay I am. If you said I was engaged to your mother I'd dare say it too. I've no idea who I am, or what I am, or what I'm saying, or doing...(II-24)

Unable to withstand the predicament any longer, Tom finally resigns himself to his fate. Intending to turn himself in he declares, "I don't care now, I've nothing to lose, and I'm a desperate man!" (III-29).

In addition to the eccentric characterizations, much of the humor derives from Gilbert's use of a substantial variety of very funny farcical diction devices. First, there is that language which stems directly from the conscious confusion of the victim. For instance, Tom sorts out the nature of his predicament in the following manner:

> TOM: There is grim justice in the fact that my punishment will be brought through the employers of the son of the husband of the mother of the young women to whom I was to have been married. (III-29, 30)

Gilbert also included a traditionally extensive use of puns and accents, but in a somewhat more sophisticated manner than Byron and others before him. For example, the following discussion of the Colonel's doubtful military career is carefully crafted in contrasting meaning, sound, and rhythm:

> TOM: What's he a Colonel of?
> COLONEL: Colonel of a Regiment, to be sure.
> TOM: Yes, but in what service?
> O'FIPP: Never mind the surrvice, sorr. It was the 27th regiment of it. That's enough for any man. There's many a surrvice besides the British surrvice, I believe, sorr?
> TOM: Oh, I believe there's a good many.
> O'FIPP: There's the Spanish surrvice, sorr—and Hungarian surrvice—and the Italian surrvice, and the French surrvice, and the—
> MATILDA: And the dinner surrvice.
> TOM: And the Church Service. (I-5)

Related to such punning is another diction device that Gilbert helped popularize in farce—name jokes. Used only occasionally in the earlier one-acts, name jokes are the mistakenly punned or mispronounced name of the victim as used by another character. When Matilda tries to explain Tom's true identity to Caroline, the following exchange occurs:

> MATILDA: Don't call him Arthur—his name's Tom—Tom.
> CAROLINE: Tomtom. Impossible. Tell them, Arthur, that it is false. Tell them that you are not—you cannot be Tomtom. (III-31)

Such diction victimization came to be used in almost every full-length farce of the nineteenth century.

Gilbert's refined use of farcical language is also evident in his extensive use of topsey-turvey nonsense. In Act I, the Colonel's disapproval of Tom is a perfect example of the device: "But that's the way with mean and thankless natures," he maintains. "Do 'em an injustice and they're never satisfied till they've retaliated" (I-12). Even the usual one-act farce ending that realigns farce with standard Victorian morality is sacrificed to the Gilbertian viewpoint. *Tom Cobb* ends on an amoral, cynical note that further demonstrates that Gilbert viewed the world of farce as reflecting more than innocent fun:

> TOM: Caroline, you loved me as a penniless, but poetical Major-General, can you still love me as a wealthy, but unromantic apothecary?
> CAROLINE: I can! I can love you as a wealthy anything!
> MRS. EFFINGHAM: We all can!
> BULSTRODE: All!...*(CURTAIN)* (III-32)

The use of spectacle in *Tom Cobb* is also integral to the Gilbertian viewpoint. Scenery and costumes are consistently used to illustrate the changing fortunes of the characters. Act I takes place in the "shabby but pretentious" sitting room of the Colonel's house. Both he and his daughter are likewise dressed in "shabby genteel clothing" (I-2). In Act II, after he has bilked Tom of his fortune, the same room is discovered to be "very handsomely furnished," and the Colonel and Matilda are "showily dressed" (I-2). Act III illustrates Tom's identity crisis by being set in the "shabbily furnished" drawing room of the Effingham house. Tom enters, completely changed in appearance: "He parts his hair in the centre, and allows it to grow long. He wears a very low lay-down collar in order to look Byronic" (III-25). Despite the central importance of scenery and costumes, the play makes little use of the traditional physical business of knockabout for farcical effect. There are no chases, no concealments, no food business, and hardly any *lazzi* having to do with doors. The only knockabout occurs in Act III when Tom becomes confused by Matilda's refusal to admit that she knows him:

> Tom: Now Matilda, don't *you* deny me?... *(puts his arm around her and kisses her. Enter Whipple R. He seizes Tom by the collar and whirls him away from Matilda.)* (II-18)

Standing alone, as it does, this single incident of physical humor seems inconsistent rather than integral to the overall farcical effect.

The critical reaction to *Tom Cobb* was as mixed as the quality of its construction. While praising its generally humorous effect, the critics called it to task for being hard to understand and for lacking a sufficient degree of victimization and a carefully plotted line of probability. The anonymous *Theatre* critic most clearly summarized this opinion:

> The whole, however, is wearisome and not too intelligible, and wants the consistency indispensable to a genuine work of art... A more comic effect might easily have been produced with the means at hand, and the elaboration of the self-begotten perplexities of the hero would have added to the probability of the play as much as to its interest.

The reviewer also suggested a distinctly Gilbertian flaw in the play by pointing out that Gilbert's "happiest results have generally been obtained when feminine wiles and lures have been the subject of satire. In his best and most successful plays, masculine selfishness is arrayed against the extravagance of feminine impulse.[29]

In his second, more famous, and only other "Entirely Original Farcical Comedy," Gilbert seems to have tried to respond to the major criticisms of *Tom Cobb*. *Engaged*, which opened at the Haymarket on October 3, 1877, deals with the classic Gilbertian female/male conflict while exhibiting some refinements in construction. On the other hand, Gilbert still failed to achieve ultimate success with the three-act intrigue form as it applied to farce. In addition, Gilbert's cynical attitude toward the farcical universe in general and human nature in particular is much more pervasive in *Engaged* than in *Tom Cobb*. Augustin Filon said of the play, "So cruel a farce had never been seen."[30]

Engaged deals with the same general sort of victimization as *Tom Cobb*. An innocent Cheviot Hill is besieged by a pack of unscrupulous, mercenary, avaricious characters who are after his potential inheritance. Unlike the plot of *Tom Cobb,* however, the plot of *Engaged* is tremendously complicated; the incidents of victimization are so numerous that the story is difficult to describe efficiently.

The victimizers, as a group, are derived from the world of topsey-turvey Victorian morality in which human activity is ruled by self-seeking ideals without regard to standards of right or wrong. In this regard Filon creatively speculated on Gilbert's thinking as he sat down to write *Engaged:*

> My dramatis personae shall be neither good nor bad, they shall be naively and absolutely selfish . . . They shall lack only moral sense; of this organ I shall deprive them as neatly and gently as possible. Fiance and Fiancee, father and daughter, friend and friend shall become enemies the moment their interests clash. The moment their interests agree they shall clasp hands and kiss again as before. Three couples will perform these evolutions and manoeuvres before the audience and the young girls will change their lovers as complacently as they would their partners in quadrille.[31]

This is not to say, however, that *Engaged* is not funny. As a farce, it works its effects exclusively through laughter, only with larger than usual doses of ridicule. Throughout, Gilbert used traditional and innovative devices for substantial humorous effect.

As the farcical victim, Cheviot Hill, like Tom Cobb, is the only character not beset by greed. But unlike Tom, Cheviot is characterized by a habitual eccentricity similar to that of the Colonel in the earlier farce: he proposes marriage to every woman he meets. Thus, in this play, Gilbert raised the plot device of the legal promise of marriage to a new level of importance. In addition, Gilbert's eccentric characterization of the farce victim became a highly influential, if not definitive, aspect of native, original, Victorian farce.

Cheviot's particular predicament is described in the following efficient exposition delivered by his financial guardian, Belvawney:

> BELVAWNEY: . . . His father (who comes of a very old family—the Cheviot Hills had settled in this part of the world centuries before the conquest) is compelled by his health to reside in Madeira. Knowing that I exercise all but supernatural influence over his son, and fearing that his affectionate disposition would lead him to contract an undesirable marriage, the old gentleman allows me 1,000 pounds a year so long as Cheviot Hill shall live single, but at his death or marriage the money goes over to Cheviot's Uncle Symperson, who is now travelling to town with him.[32]

Thus the basic plot complication has Cheviot pledging his undying love to one girl just as another is about to catch his fancy: "I am quite determined," he proclaims in typical fashion, "that nothing shall shake my constancy to Minnie. *(enter Parker, D. F. R.)* What a devilish pretty girl!" (II-26).

As in *Tom Cobb* Gilbert was at his best with the invention of clever farcical dialogue. In addition to his humorous use of puns, name jokes, and dialects, with *Engaged* Gilbert popularized recurring dialogue, raised the stream-of-conscious confusion to near elegance, and developed what may be called the farcical undercut to embody his topsey-turvy viewpoint. Recurring dialogue, which appeared occasionally in afterpiece farce, is the repetition of obviously identical lines by the victim as he confronts similar predicaments throughout the dramatic action; Gilbert used this device to good effect in *Engaged.* Each time Cheviot meets a new girl he enthusiastically declares, "Madame, be not surprised when I tell you that I cannot resist the conviction that you are the light of my future life, the essence of every hope, the tree upon which the fruit of my heart is growing—my past, my present, my future, my own to come!" (I-18). This recurring dialogue proved so funny in *Engaged* that hardly a single famous British farce from *The Private Secretary* to *Charley's Aunt* fails to use the device successfully. The stream-of-conscious confusion, which one-act farceurs such as Morton used effectively, was endowed by Gilbert with rhythmic and musical qualities that rendered its use desperately elegant. In the following example Miss Treherne, having received the standard marriage proposal from Cheviot, wrestles with the illogic of her predicament:

> MISS TREHERNE: Fun! Say, rather, horror-distraction... I am rent with conflicting doubts! Perhaps he was already married; in that case I am a bigamist. Maybe he is dead; in that case, I am a widow. Maybe he is alive; in that case I am a wife. What am I? Am I single? Am I married? Am I a widow? Can I marry? Have I married? May I marry? Who am I? Where am I? What am I? What is my name? What is my condition in life? If I am married, to whom am I married? If I am a widow, how came I to be a widow, and whose widow came I to be? Why am I his widow? What did he die of? Did he leave me anything? If any thing, how much, and is it saddled with conditions?—Can I marry again without forfeiting it? Have I a mother-in-law? Have I a family of step-children, and if so, how many, and what are their ages, sexes, sizes, names and dispositions? These are questions that rack me night and day, and until they are settled, peace and I are not on terms! (II-24)

For his most direct statement of inverted Victorian values, Gilbert developed the farcical undercut. An expansion of the inverted one-liner, it consists of an extensive scene or speech of demonstrated or declared morality or sentiment which is undercut at its most sincere point by an obviously farcical joke, either visual or verbal. Such a device is a perfect means of revealing the mercenary motivations behind each character's loftier sentiments. Miss Treherne again provides the salient example as she declares her love for Belvawney:

MISS TREHERNE: Belvawney, all this is quite true, I love you madly, passionately, I dare to live but in your heart, I breathe but for your love; yet, before I actually consent to take the irrevocable step that will place me in the pinnacle of my fondest hopes, you must give me some definite idea of your pecuniary position. I am not mercenary, heaven knows; but business is business, and I confess I should like a little definite information about the settlements. (I-8)

The farcical undercut was yet another Gilbertian device that became a definitive aspect of full-length British farces—especially those of Pinero and of the writers of the so-called extreme farces.[33]

Gilbert used physical business for humorous effect much more extensively in *Engaged* than in *Tom Cobb*—*lazzi* that ranged from food business to fantasy spectacle. In one scene Gilbert undercuts the sincerity of Miss Treherne's pretended joy at meeting her rival, Minnie, by having her eat tarts all through their embraces. At other points the action calls for simple sight gags such as the following:

(Cheviot places a hole with his finger through newspaper and reconnoitres unobserved... Maggie advances to hole in newspaper and peeps through.) (II-33)

Undoubtedly influenced by the success of his extravaganzas, Gilbert introduced an element of fantasy into his eccentric characterizations. In this instance Gilbert endowed Belvawney's eyes with the magical power of control over Cheviot's actions—a power that Cheviot tries at all costs to avoid:

CHEVIOT: You know the strange, mysterious influence that his eyes exercise over me.... They are much inflamed just now, and he has to wear green spectacles. Whilst this lasts I am a free agent, but under treatment they may recover. In that case, if he knew that I contemplated matrimony, he would use them to prevent my doing so—and I cannot resist them—I cannot resist them! (I-12)

Unlike some of Gilbert's other innovative contributions to British farce, elements of fantasy or the supernatural never caught on with subsequent farceurs. Perhaps this is owing to the fact that supernatural causality detracts from the seemingly realistic universality of the farcical predicament.

Overall, Gilbert substantially improved his handling of characterization and the farce devices of diction and spectacle in his second original farce. Like *Tom Cobb*, however, *Engaged* fails in the area of Gilbert's awkward handling of the intrigue structure as applied to the three-act farce. Despite the fact that *Engaged* contains a significantly larger number of major plot complications than *Tom Cobb* (thirty versus twelve) the overall sense of desperation is diminished. As a result, the plot machinery becomes strikingly noticeable and the farcical coincidence that keeps the action moving appears merely as illogic and improbability. The lack of desperation likely derives in part from the use of an early point of attack (the action is spread over four months) and from Gilbert's failure to use such devices as the chase or significantly truncated time. In addition, the distribution of action among the acts is inefficient. Act II, for instance, is almost totally superfluous. Made up of episodic proposals by Cheviot, the situation at the end of the act is not appreciably different from that at its beginning. It fails to heighten the sense of victimization and could be either dispensed with entirely or substantially edited and tacked on to one of the other two acts.

Public and critical reaction to this entirely original farce was mixed at best. *Engaged* had a rather short initial run, although there were at least three moderately successful revivals in 1878, 1881, and 1886. In a review of the 1878 revival Clement Scott summed up the critical reaction to the play, which ranged from dour appreciation to just plain boredom:

> Opinions differed very widely as to the merits of Mr. W. S. Gilbert's *Engaged* when that farcical comedy was originally produced. Whilst some were found to relish the curious subacid flavour of the plot, with its inverted motives, its perpetual satire, and its strange combination of prosaic realism and utter absurdity, others were heard to cry out against its heartlessness and needless cynicism. Some, again, who did not complain of the spirit of the play, objected to it simply on the ground of its being dull and full of repetition; they failed to appreciate its humour, and could not imagine why such story as it possessed could not have been told in a couple of acts. [34]

Filon, however, saw a more deep-rooted, distinctively Gilbertian reason for its ultimate failure with the public. Noting that the theatre-going populace had always accepted farces in which two or at most three characters were ridiculed, he points out that Gilbert caricatured all mankind. The audiences laughed, but the overall jest was just too bitter to swallow; it was at the same time too unreal and too true. While such cynical outspokenness might be suitable for the denizens of some dreamland, "it was incongruous where people travelled by railway and read the paper." [35] In other words, the public could readily accept the Gilbertian viewpoint only when it was distanced by the fantasy of the Savoy operas.

Gilbert's efforts at entirely original farcical comedy writing went unimitated throughout the 1870s. His works were not good models for British playwrights who had little practical experience at efficiently organizing farcical action over the course of three acts. And organization, as Eric Bentley notes, must be the essential talent of the full-length farceur:

> He who organizes a whole evening of merriment must indeed be an organizer...Nothing could be more fatal than to stake all on making a good beginning and then let events take their course...and it is something every author of a farce must have in mind—or better in his bones. [36]

Accordingly, the inexperienced British playwrights turned again to their mentors in one-act farcical construction—the French, who had a ready repertoire of models ripe for translation, adaptation, and inspiration. Over the next ten years the production of full-length farces adapted from the French became one of the most lucrative theatrical enterprises ever seen in England.

2

Farcical Comedies
Adapted from the French

There is a tradition that the director of the Princess's had a tame translator under lock and key who turned French into English without respite, his chain never loosened nor his hunger satisfied until his task, for the time being, should be complete.
—P. M. Augustin Filon

That British playwrights and managers should turn to the French was not only the continuation of a profitable farce tradition, it was also logical. The British had only an afterpiece tradition of farce, whereas the French had perfected the full-length form in the early nineteenth century. As with the mid-century *vaudeville,* the full-length French farces were adapted voraciously by the British. Of the ninety-four farcical comedies produced in London in the years 1875–1883 almost two-thirds were adapted from French originals.[1]

Also, as in the days of the one-act farces, British copyright law facilitated the adaptation of the longer versions. In 1875 Parliament passed a law that brought adaptations under the same ineffective legal strictures as translations. Under the new laws, a foreign author owned his work internationally for only five years, after which it entered the free public domain. This law remained in effect and unamended for twelve years, encouraging adaptation.

The primary targets of the British adapters were the so-called "well-made plays" that were popularized by Eugène Scribe and promoted by his disciples, Victorien Sardou and Eugène Labiche.

The Well-Made Play

Scribe was one of the most prolific playwrights of all time. He wrote a total of 374 dramatic works, including 216 one-act *comédies-vaudevilles,* thirty-five full-length plays, libretti for twenty-eight operas, eighty-six *opéras-*

comiques, and nine *opéras-ballets.* This output was facilitated by the fact that Scribe constructed dramatic action according to a specific formula. Scribe, however, did not invent his dramaturgical methods. Rather he perfected a system of cause-and-effect plotting that goes back to the time of Sophocles. It yielded a type of play so efficient in its structuring that it earned the designation *pièce bien fait* or "well-made play." The typical well-made play had the following structural aspects: (1) a short, efficient *exposition* in which the major characters are introduced and all necessary information about their backgrounds is presented; followed by (2) *incidents of complication* that are related through cause and effect that usually take the form of misunderstandings, lost papers, intercepted messages and secrets which cannot be revealed; which all suspensefully lead up to (3) *the obligatory scene (scène à faire).* Containing the crisis or turning point of the action, the obligatory scene is the inevitable confrontation of misunderstandings that is at once the lowest and highest point in the protagonist's adventure. It is followed by (4) the *dénouement* or the unravelling of the plot which is accomplished as quickly as possible, usually involving a sensational last-minute revelation that permits (5) a logical *resolution,* often involving a spectacular conversion. In multiple-act plays this pattern is repeated to a degree in all but the last act, each ending with a suspenseful reversal that hints at ultimate disaster.

Throughout the plot of the well-made play, the cause-and-effect progression of the incidents is facilitated by coincidence that is dependent upon a clever and precise manipulation of dramatic irony. Probably no literary medium can better use its means to achieve a high degree of irony than drama, owing primarily to the silent presence of the audience. Audiences are, in fact, part and parcel of the very definition of irony:

> Irony is a form of utterance that postulates a double audience, consisting of one party that hearing shall hear and shall not understand, and another party that, when more is meant than meets the ear, is aware both of that more and of the outsiders' incomprehension.[2]

The principal irony device of the well-made play was what the French referred to as a *quiproquo* (literally, a misunderstanding, mistake, or misapprehension) and the English referred to as an *equivoque.* In practice this device incorporated at least two characters who interpret a word or situation in different ways, all the time assuming that their interpretations are the same.

Despite the fact that the action-oriented, well-made play is currently viewed derisively as trite and unoriginal, nineteenth-century critics viewed Scribe as an innovator and consistently praised his impeccable craftsmanship.

In England the well-made play first began to appear in translations of Scribe's sentimental comedies. Translations of his vaudevilles appeared at the

Olympic Theatre in the 1830s and proceeded to influence the whole generation of afterpiece farceurs at mid-century. In the forties and fifties the influence of the full-length well-made play is evident in the works of Edward Bulwer-Lytton, Tom Taylor, and significantly, T. W. Robertson. When Robertson's first produced play, *A Night's Adventure* (1851), proved unsuccessful, he turned successfully to translating and adapting French well-made plays, such as *The Ladies' Battle* (1851) from *La bataille des dames* by Scribe and Legouvé and *A Glass of Water* from Scribe's famous *Un verre d'eau*. After thoroughly schooling himself in the well-made play technique, Robertson was finally able to achieve success with his own realistic plays by applying Scribe's formula to the domestic elements of Victorian middle-class life.

Scribe's primary disciples in France were Victorien Sardou and Eugène Labiche. With a dramatic range almost as wide as Scribe's, Sardou wrote farces, comedies, historical dramas, melodramas, and problem plays. Labiche specialized almost exclusively in farce and light comedy. Labiche used the well-made play structure to achieve successively bigger laughs instead of more sensational suspense. His most famous farce, *The Italian Straw Hat* (1861) *(Un chapeau de paille d'Italie)* is a prime example. In this farce, a young man is plunged into a progressively more difficult predicament when his horse happens to eat the hat of a woman who should have been somewhere else at the time. The poor man is thus forced into a desperate chase trying to find an identical replacement before her husband "discovers all." In 1873 William Schwenck Gilbert's translation of *An Italian Straw Hat* as *The Wedding March* achieved success at the Court Theatre, finally demonstrating the farcical possibilities of the three-act form.

The Pink Dominos Sensation

A more lasting influence on British farceurs, however, came from the sensational adaptation of Alfred Hennequin's and Alfred Delacour's *Les dominos roses* (1876) as *The Pink Dominos* (1877) by James Albery. It was his adaptation upon which almost all British farce was modelled for the next ten years.

James Albery (1838–1886) was an unlikely candidate for such a distinction. In his time he was generally recognized as a successor to Robertson. Thus, Albery's most famous original play was of the cup and saucer variety, a sentimental comedy titled *Two Roses* that brought initial success to Henry Irving in 1870. Like Byron, Albery wrote a variety of humorous and comic forms from light witty pieces to one-act farces and extravaganzas. Archer, among others, found him hard to categorize:

> I should like, in conclusion, to sum up Mr. Albery's literary character in a neatly rounded paragraph, but it somehow does not lend itself readily to neatly rounded treatment. It is too full of contradictions and paradoxes.[3]

The major flaw in Albery's original works was his inability to construct full-length, well-made plots—a typically British shortcoming of the time. To circumvent the problem, Albery turned to the French in 1877 for what was to be his first in a long line of farcical adaptations.

For this initial effort Albery chose to adapt *Les dominos roses,* which had already achieved great success in its Paris run and in a sensational New York opening at the Adelphi Theatre in an adaptation by Dion Boucicault called *Forbidden Fruit* (1876). Albery's version, *The Pink Dominos,* opened at the Criterion Theatre in March of 1877 and was equally successful. It played for 555 consecutive performances, distinguishing it as the longest running British farce up to that time.

The success of *The Pink Dominos* was due partly to its efficient structure, but more to the fact that it was the first three-act farce adaptation to include what the British considered French "risqué" cynicism. *The Pink Dominos* follows the same basic story and sequence of complications as the original. In *Les dominos roses* two married men secretly plan an evening on the town with ladies of racy reputation. They agree to meet at a restaurant known for a rather risqué primary trade other than serving food. The set, of course, requires a number of doors that lead to "private" rooms. The major complication of the play occurs when the men's wives coincidentally arrive at the same restaurant, to the men's utter befuddlement and horror. The desperation builds as the action climaxes with all the characters chasing and hiding among the doors. The play ends with the reconciliation of husbands and wives at home—after a difficult and painful unravelling. In this French version, the marital infidelity is not only intended, but nearly committed by all.

By contrast, in the English version, it is the titillating *suspicion* of infidelity by the characters that keeps the action complicated. The audience, and eventually the characters, are aware that no wickedness was actually committed. In *The Pink Dominos* the two husbands, unassuming Charles Greythorne and Percey Waggstaffe, make an unplanned rendezvous at the restaurant with two mysterious women in pink dominos.[4] The women are their wives who have secretly set out to test their husbands' devotion. Both couples proceed to engage in a wild sequence of complications almost identical to those in *Les dominos roses.* The coincidental nature of the original assignation and the fact that the unknown temptresses are the wives ultimately renders the complications of *The Pink Dominos* harmless. In Act III, the characters sort out the mix-up more efficiently than in the French version since only the clarifying of identity, and not intentions, is necessary. Thus, it was the suspicion, the implication, and the momentary temptation of improperly risqué behavior—which had not been seen in British humorous drama since the Restoration—that titillated the Victorian theatregoers; in the preceding mid-century period of *vaudeville* adaptation, not even a suggestion of impropriety was acceptable.

While the so-called "deodorizing" of *The Pink Dominos* made the play more acceptable than it would have been earlier, the most visible aspects of Victorianism were strongly in evidence. Accordingly, in the adaptation Victorian morality demanded that wives forgive their husbands' momentary lapses as Lady Maggie recommends at the conclusion:

> LADY MAGGIE: Do you remember the legend of the Priest entering the temple and finding a little ass seated by the god and afterwards out of respect to the deity the priest always entered blindfolded. This is why you must worship at the shrine of your husband's virtue! Deliberately blindfold yourself and then you will not see the ugly little beast . . . let this be your first lesson: follow my example and don't ask. It will save your husband a fib.[5]

The popularity of veiled titillation with the public was tempered somewhat by the severely negative reactions of the conservative critics who longed for the good old days. The most vociferous in condemnation was, expectedly, Clement Scott. In his scathing *Daily Telegraph* review, he bitterly deplored the new method of adapting French farces:

> Parisian dramatists are by no means squeamish about the modes they adopt to excite the merriment of not over-fastidious audiences, and when the ingenuity of their plots has tempted the English adapter to appropriate the fruits of their invention a kind of deodorizing process has been usually deemed necessary before presentation to a London public of a theatrical dish compounded by such ingredients. This wholesome precaution has certainly been discarded in reference to "The Pink Dominos," translated by Mr. James Albery from "Les Dominos Roses." . . . Of the very nature of the story it would hardly be excessive prudishness to withhold a description, for the same reason that no one in a family circle would think of explicitly detailing the plots of the plays of the Restoration.[6]

Significantly, however, not all of London's critics deplored *The Pink Dominos*. Before Scott began to write reviews for *The Theatre*, that journal's anonymous critic praised Albery's play as "a capital instance of successful adaptation. In some respects, indeed, it is better than the original. The last act is a model of construction . . . If not exactly childlike in innocence, the intrigue in 'The Pink Dominos' has at least, no absolute wickedness."[7]

Coupled with the public appetite for farce, such favorable evaluation was all that was needed for theatrical entrepreneurs to justify their new rush to acquire adaptations of French farces. In fact, by the end of the run of *The Pink Dominos* the advertising of a farce "from the French" became a bigger guarantee of a draw than did "entirely original."

The French Farce "Deodorized"

The major authors adapting French farces in the manner of *The Pink Dominos* were all of a type: they were prolific writers of humorous forms who relied heavily on foreign sources to supplement their original work. The most productive writer in this period was Francis Cowley Burnand. Born in 1836, Burnand wrote his first play, a one-act farce, while a schoolboy at Eton. As a professional dramatist, he went on to write 150 plays of which thirteen were adapted farcical comedies. The most successful of these was *Betsy* (1879) adapted from *Bébé* (1877) by Hennequin and de Najac. The most famous adaptor was Sidney Grundy (1848–1914), who contributed nine farcical comedies out of his total of over fifty plays. All but one of his farces were adapted from foreign sources.

Next to *The Pink Dominos* the most successful farce of the period was Grundy's *The Snowball* (1879), adapted from Scribe's *Oscar, ou le mari qui tromp sa femme* (1861). Other successful adaptor/farceurs of the period include H. J. Byron, who wrote 4 farcical comedies out of a total output of 143 plays, Robert Reece (7 farcical comedies out of 108 plays), and George Sims (7 farces out of 49 plays).

The primary sources for their adaptations were the farces of Scribe, Sardou, and Labiche, and to a lesser degree those of Hennequin, Delacour, de Najac, Courteline, Bisson, and Pailleron.

The British farceurs used the example of *The Pink Dominos* for their adaptations. They carefully followed the basic sequence of well-made complications in the originals and substantially "deodorized" the French morality so as to leave a vestige of suggestiveness. As in *The Pink Dominos* and *The Wedding March* the common subject matter was seeming adultery. The typical plot was a kind of domestic misadventure that titillated through misunderstandings instead of the actual deceptions of the French originals. In addition to the equivocal nature of the plot, this deodorization *cum* titillation can be seen at each structural level of these farcical comedies.

The most apparent adapting is evident in the creation of the characters, especially the women. Inevitably the married French woman became the single English girl. Although such a change succeeded in maintaining Victorian propriety, it did not always serve the best dramatic purposes. In his review of *Themis* (1880), which was adapted from Sardou's *Les pommes de Monsieur Voisin,* Ernest A. Bendall pointed out that the farcical comedy "seems in the process of adaptation to have lost much of its original point, as is often the case with plays in which an unmarried heroine is substituted for that favorite character of the French state, the risky [*sic*] married woman."[8] In a major editorial in *The Theatre,* Clement Scott explained the Victorian social basis for such a change:

French society and English society, though only separated by the Channel, are as wide apart as if the Atlantic or Pacific Ocean flowed between. In France a girl begins her life when she is married; In England she ends it. This is the vital difference. The dramas of adultery so popular in France and so detested in England may be traced to this absorbing fact.[9]

Thus, the major change involved in making a British farcical comedy from a French one was an alteration of the domestic, social viewpoint of the original. In the French originals, once the farcical complications destroyed domestic tranquility, it was never quite re-established. In the farcical comedies, however, the ending always reaffirmed the opening picture of familial harmony by the simple clarification of a misunderstanding as opposed to the discovery of an actual moral transgression.

Unlike the French originals there are no verbal improprieties in the Victorian adaptations. The public would surely have been offended by their use on stage and thus the official censors guarded against it, often demanding many word changes in the farcical comedies submitted for licensing. Filon described the process: "Where our authors have had the effrontery to write the word 'cocotte' in black and white, they replace it by the word 'actress'. Where we have unblushingly written 'adultery' they have inserted 'flirtation.'"[10]

Still, times were changing, and in the wave of titillating farcical comedies that were produced, playwrights sought to thinly disguise their language and their characters' actions, a practice that critics like Scott never approved: "In the grand history of humbug," he wrote, "a chapter ought to be devoted to the plays written to titillate, and the audiences pretending not to catch the meaning, but laughing behind their fans."[11]

For an adaptation to avoid being labeled "humbug" all potentially illicit actions, characters, thoughts, and dialogue had to be rendered—inevitably—innocent. F. C. Burnand performed the operation successfully by transforming the French *Bébé* into the very popular British *Betsy* in 1879 at the Criterion. In the original, the protagonist is the young knave, Gaston, son of a baron, who is treated as a child. Secretly, however, he is romantically and sexually quite experienced, having had several affairs with young women, the wife of a family friend, and the family maid, Toinette. The farcical action is resolved when Gaston's sexual maturity is discovered, and the family friend is convinced not to suspect his wife (who had actually been seduced by Gaston). In the end, Gaston is forced to marry his distant cousin, Bébé. For *Betsy*, Burnand maintained the sequence of complications and some of the dialogue from the original, but radically altered the characters and their relationships to one another. In the adaptation Adolphus (Gaston) only has eyes for Nellie, a perfectly respectable young girl. Completing the farcical triangle, the maid, Betsy, wants only to marry Adolphus, not to have an affair with him. Thus, intimations of sexual infidelity are totally absent in *Betsy*. Even the unfaithful

Figure 5. Final Scene from the Original Production of F.C. Burnand's *Betsy*, 1879
(Illustrated Sporting and Dramatic News)

wife in the original is changed into the unmarried Madame Polenta, an eccentric voice teacher.

The critical reaction to *Betsy* was overwhelmingly favorable. Even Clement Scott praised it, refusing to take offense at the veiled raciness:

> To those who like lively reckless nonsense and are unfamiliar with MM. Henequin and Najac's highly entertaining, if extremely improper *Bébé*, Mr. Burnand's *Betsy* will doubtless appear to be a satisfactory work of its kind ... it reflects much credit alike upon his ingenious manipulation and upon the purity of his taste.[12]

As Scott's evaluation implies, it was not only the deodorized prurience that made the French-style farcical comedies so popular. Rather it was the more traditional fact that they were stuffed with plenty to keep the audience laughing. Simply stated, the English enjoyed the very funny, farcical efficiency of the well-made play.

As in *Tom Cobb* and *Engaged* the early native varieties of full-length farce were not only morally tame compared to the adaptations, they were also structurally awkward in the distribution of farcical complications over three acts. The first and most outspoken British playwright to publicly advocate the use of the well-made form in native farcical comedies was not Albery or Burnand, but Sidney Grundy.

Grundy's first plays, like those of other farce writers of the period, were humorous one-acts, including two farces, *On Change* (1872) and *Reading for the Bar* (1876), and a commedietta, *All at Sea* (1873).[13] His first full-length work was a Byron-type comedy called *Mammon* (1877). What gave him sudden success and started his dramatic career off in a new direction was his adaptation of a Scribe farce that was produced at the Strand on February 18, 1879, as *The Snowball*.

Grundy praised his mentor, Scribe, in an article titled "Dramatic Construction," published in *The Theatre* of April 1, 1881. Grundy began by declaring flatly that "Construction is the most difficult, as it is the most important element in playwriting." He went on to maintain that "to a great extent both authors and critics seem to have lost sight of construction, in England, in the present day." The solution, Grundy recommended, was to sit at the feet of Scribe, "the great apostle of construction."[14] He concluded the article by quite expectedly attesting to the legitimate art of adapting:

> It is only the adapter who pulls one of them [Scribe's plays] to pieces, for the purpose of constructing a new and original play out of the component parts, who is able fully to appreciate the art of this marvellous workman. Woe betide the rash man who takes a single entrance in vain, who makes light of the most (apparently) trifling exit, who ventures to despise the slightest incident! If he removes one brick, he must reconstruct the entire edifice.[15]

Like everything else of a dramatic nature taken from the French, the structural perfection of *The Snowball* and other well-made farcical comedies was uniquely British in many respects.

For the British the final goal of their adaptations was laughter—as much as could be produced in three acts. Aside from the nature of the titillation, the primary difference between the appropriate pleasure of the French farces and the English versions is the nature of that laughter. The spirit of the French laughter was cynical, while that of the British conveyed only a sense of friendly, wholesome fun. In *The Snowball* Grundy used the final speech of direct address to remind both the audience and the critics of the sole intention of his and other farcical comedies. The speech is delivered by the actress playing Mrs. Featherstone, wife of the protagonist:

> MRS. FEATHERSTONE *(comes C. to audience):*
> We do not strive to move your hearts to tears—
> To ride the whirlwind, or to shake the spheres;
> Our humbler aim in all we do and say,
> Is just to while an idle hour away.
> Say, have we done so? If not we must try
> To suit your humour better by and by:
> But if we have, we'll leave to your controlling
> The little "Snowball" we have now set rolling.[16]

Favorable reviews of the farcical comedies in this period praised them highly for their laughter-producing qualities. The fact that contemporary reviewers like Clement Scott, E. A. Bendall, E. L. Blanchard, and Joseph Knight had good words to say about the production of British farces is highly significant; they were the first critics to praise the form since the Restoration.[17] Their reviews constitute the first body of English dramatic criticism not only to recognize but also to praise the pure entertainment, nondidactic purpose of farce.

E. A. Bendall was one of the first to accept the arousal of laughter as a legitimate critical premise. He wrote of an anonymous Sardou adaptation: "*Themis* obtains abundant laughter, and thus fairly justifies its existence."[18] A year later, in reviewing two farcical comedy adaptations by George Sims, *The Member for Slocum* (1881) and *The Mother-in-law* (1881), Bendall went a critical step further by excusing faults in the acting and writing by claiming, "But what does it matter when both plays are so laughable?—which seems to be the main point of (farcical) comedy production nowadays."[19]

The most perceptive remarks on the value of laughter in general, and in farce in particular, came from the arch-enemy of obscenity, Clement Scott. In his review of E. G. ("Robert Reece") Lankester's *The Guv'nor* (1880), Scott became one of the first to measure the quality of a play by its laughter-producing ability:

Thousands of people like plays of "The Guv'nor" class, and it is an excellent specimen of its kind. It is a play of complication and farcical mystification; and in the art of vigorous construction, so as to sustain the interest and keep up the fun, we have here a masterpiece . . . If Mr. E. G. Lankester, whoever he may be, can give us another play like this, it will be as welcome as it is appreciated. It can do nobody any harm, and it will make everybody laugh. Let no one believe that a three-act farce cannot produce art.[20]

As Gilbert had discovered in his efforts at constructing original farcical comedies, making everybody laugh was not a simple task. Whereas Gilbert had sacrificed a tightly constructed intrigue plot to the inclusion of highly eccentric characterizations, vigorous construction of the well-made adaptations yielded action-dominated farces. In his essay on construction Grundy emphasized the importance of letting no other dramatic element intrude on the design of the action:

The great lesson to be learnt from Scribe is the supreme importance of getting along with the story. This I take it, is the first principle of true construction. It sounds very simple, but how much does it mean? It means that you must not stop even to portray character, except so far as the character concerns the plot; it means that the most brilliant line ever written is bad in art if its delivery impedes the action of the play.[21]

The typical well-made farcical comedy plot involves a traditional victimization that grows through a series of absurd complications and pyramiding misunderstandings. The action is resolved when the misunderstandings are clarified. The most popular subject depicts a married man who is victimized by a series of embarrassing domestic complications invariably involving his wife, his uncle, or his aunt. Misunderstood by all around him, he is forced to the breaking point, where a crisis involving the total *dramatis personae* quickly resolves his predicament. In Lankester's *The Guv'nor,* the fifty-year-old Mr. Butterscotch mistakenly suspects his twenty-six-year-old wife of infidelity, which leads to an almost indescribable series of misunderstandings concerning his wife's faithfulness and the marital intentions of his children. In Byron's *Uncle* (1879) the young husband, Paul Beaumont, is supported financially by his millionaire uncle who is off in India—on the sole condition that he *not* get married. When his uncle makes a startling, unannounced visit, Paul desperately tries to pass off his own wife as the wife of his friend and rival, Fletcher. In Grundy's *The Snowball,* Felix Featherstone and his wife go separately to see the racy play *The Pink Dominos.* Secretly, they each see the other in the audience. Unaware that he has been discovered, Felix returns home first and contrives a trap for his wife's naughty behavior: he puts a note in her sewing basket that says he knows everything and demands to see her. However, with the aid of her sister and the maid, Mrs. Featherstone turns the tables and makes it appear that the note means that Mr. Featherstone is having an affair with the maid. The action proceeds as everyone threatens Felix with informing his wife of what he has not done. Therefore, his misery and desperation increase like a snowball rolling down a mountain.[22]

The disposition of such action over the course of three acts invariably follows the well-made intrigue plan. In Act I the opening exposition, while efficiently handled, is not the all-inclusive summary speech of the one-acts, but a longer dialogue (usually between a servant and the victim) that could be accommodated by the greater length. The exposition is followed immediately by an inciting incident that, in traditional farce fashion, begins to complicate undeservedly the victim's life. The unexpected return of Beaumont's inflexible uncle in *Uncle,* Butterscotch's coincidental discovery of a man's overcoat in *The Guv'nor,* and the innocent ambiguity of Featherstone's misdelivered note to his wife in *The Snowball* all qualify as such inciting incidents.

There is a certain aspect of expectation and dramatic irony developed in such opening incidents that is unique to farce. The very fact that a play was advertised as a farcical comedy raised the probability—in fact, the certainty— in the minds of the audience that things would turn upside down. Unlike other genres of well-made plays in which Act I is devoted to exposition and characterization with usually only one major reversal at the end of the act, the French-style farcical comedies contained a substantial number of complications in the first act. *Uncle,* for instance, contains six major plot complications in Act I; *The Snowball* contains eight, *Betsy* has nine, and *The Guv'nor* has ten. Such is the domination of action in these farces.

The overwhelming majority of the complications in these farcical comedies display similar characteristics. They stem from misunderstandings caused as two or more characters consistently make discoveries based on wrong reasoning—misunderstandings that must ultimately be reversed. The misunderstandings are connected in a linear cause-and-effect manner that is dependent on a precise manipulation of coincidental events (e.g., both husband and wife separately sneak off to the same theatre in *The Snowball*); coincidental characters (e.g., in *The Guv'nor* a dimwit who has the same name as Kate's unknown fiancé turns up to apply for a servant's job at her father's house); and coincidental objects (e.g., the ambiguous notes in *The Snowball*). Grundy emphasized the exactness required in plotting the antecedent/ consequence nature of complications:

> Effect follows cause with logical precision; each little effect becomes itself a cause, and the continually growing group is always tending toward the great effect, namely the solution of the problem or the demonstration of the theorem which is the subject matter of the play. So logical is the process, and so neat the manipulation, that there is about the complete work the same sort of beauty that there is about some of the propositions of Euclid.[23]

The usual device of misunderstanding used in the farcical comedies is the *equivoque,* an ambiguous word or phrase, written or spoken, having two or more meanings. The most common form of farcical comedy equivocation is a variation of the simple declaration, "I know all!" In *The Guv'nor,* for instance, Lankester uses the equivoque no fewer than sixteen times in complicating the action. Typical of the equivocation in *The Guv'nor* is the following mistaken assumption by the victim, Butterscotch:

> MRS. MACCLESFIELD: No doubt sir, you are right, But you must make allowances for their conduct, when you know that they love each other to distraction!
> BUTTERSCOTCH: Good heavens, madam! Then you know all about it? *(retreats)*[24]

Of course, Butterscotch and Mrs. Macclesfield each have a different loving couple in mind. Finally frustrated by his increasing inability to communicate clear information, Butterscotch blurts out the ultimate equivoque near the end of the play: "I want no equivocation—your friend has confided all to me!" (III-44).

In *The Snowball,* Grundy worked a clever variation on the equivoque by having the victim's wife, Mrs. Featherstone, order Penelope, the maid, to frighten her husband into action with the horrifying threat, "I'll tell everything!" Penelope has no idea what the phrase refers to, but she is clever enough in seeing its effect to turn it to her own use in blackmailing Featherstone and his wife by threatening to tell this "everything" she does not know. It is only the audience, with dramatic irony on its side, that actually knows "everything."

The first major reversal in the farcical comedies—a suspense device— occurs at the end of the first act. At the end of Act I of *The Snowball,* Felix Featherstone has just convinced Penelope not to tell his wife "everything" when his Uncle John, who suspects he is having an affair with the maid, enters:

> FEATHERSTONE: I beg your pardon—I will raise your wages—I'll do anything—if you will only promise not to tell my wife.
> *(Re-enter Uncle John; he stands thunderstruck.)*
> UNCLE JOHN: *Well! (Penelope looks up, sees Uncle John, gives a light shriek and runs out, L. Felix rises in consternation, turns and sees him standing R. of table.)*
> FEATHERSTONE: Uncle John! *(ring curtain)*
> UNCLE JOHN: If I had any doubt before, this settles it! *(curtain descends quickly. Picture- Quick drop.)* (I-17)

The snowball is off and rolling faster than ever.

It is Act II of these farcical comedies that is stuffed with the most farcical complications. By comparison it contains on the average one and a half to two times as many complications as do either Act I or Act III. For instance, in *Uncle* the ratio by act is 6–14–9, in *The Snowball* it is 8–18–8, in *Betsy* it is 9–27–17, and in *The Guv'nor* it is 10–16–9. It is usually Act II, therefore, that contains the most frenetic, desperate action. The majority of the chases, knockabout, and other physical harassment of the victim occurs in this act. The curtain complication of Act II is invariably the most spectacularly disastrous. It seems to plunge the victim into irretrievable hopelessness, not unlike the cliff-hanger of cinematic serial melodramas. For example, Act II of *The Snowball* is practically one long, frenetic chase, as Felix Featherstone tries to escape being pinned with another incriminating note.

Despite the fullness of Act II, it is the third acts of these farcical comedies that are most complex and undoubtedly difficult to construct. Not only does the action have to be picked up after the frenetic second act, but it also has to be resolved; all of the numerous misunderstandings must be clarified. Act III usually begins with a sort of post-Act II exposition which deflates the disaster of the previous act's ending. It also provides background on a few new characters who are usually introduced into the intrigue at this point. Such mid-action exposition usually includes a speech of recapitulation by the victim that, delivered desperately, serves as a valuable reminder to the audience of the exact status of his complicated predicament. In this fashion, Birkett, the victim in *Betsy,* responds to Mrs. McMannus' question, "What's the matter?"

> BIRKETT: Matter! You ask what's the matter. From the moment you came here, everything's gone wrong. You get my son into a difficulty; you get me into a difficulty; you go hiding about all over the place. I can't explain why you're here, or why you're there, and if I did, your husband's as mad as a hatter, and is all over the place slaying everybody—and it's all you—you—and you calmly ask me what's the matter.[25]

After the new exposition, the action resumes as the misunderstandings continue to multiply, plunging the victim deeper into his predicament. The number and sequence of complications in Act III, however, are not nearly as numerous or as frenetic as they were in Act II. To duplicate the stuffing of Act II would be unsatisfying, even unbearable; some relief is needed. In this vein, George M. Cohan's famous partner, Sam H. Harris, once knowingly criticized a Kaufman and Hart farce by observing, "the third act is too noisy."[26]

The problems of resolving a farce are several. First, because of its sole purpose of having fun and arousing laughter, the farceur is led to wait until the very last minute to create the obligatory scene. Such structuring is practical, since an earlier crisis only provides the opportunity for a moral, sentimental rationalization or explanation of previous happenings. Second, it is conceivably more difficult to write a happy ending to a highly complicated action-oriented play than the kind of catastrophic ending used in domestic tragedies and melodramas of the period. Leading farce actor-author, Charles Hawtrey, reflected on this problem in his autobiography:

> It is the most difficult thing in the world to work out a happy ending to a play and at the same time avoid the commonplace. Conversely it is the easiest thing in the world to kill off your hero, or your heroine. What puzzles me is that it is always regarded as proof of originality to end a play with a death![27]

Third, and most difficult, is the sheer problem of having to resolve so many complications involving so many characters. In effect, finally telling and knowing all is the most difficult structural task facing the writer of an equivocation farce.

Actually, the British solution to the three-act farce resolution was as efficient as it was traditional. Using a device such as a dinner party in order to get all of the characters together, an outside, previously unknown source intervenes to end the predicament, summarily and capriciously—much in the manner in which it was originally incited. In *Betsy,* when it appears as if Adolphus is going to have to marry the maid against his will because of his written promise on the back of her photograph, it is suddenly discovered that the declaration was written by Betsy's old boyfriend in the army. In Gilbert's *On Bail,* the victim, Lovibond, has been undeservedly thrown into jail. Desperate, he resorts to violence, when the jailer suddenly enters with the summary explanation that the jury threw out his case. In *Uncle,* the resolution is even less complicated. The truth about Beaumont's predicament and all mistaken identities is learned by his uncle while offstage. Beaumont's confusion and his uncle's advice are typical disclaimers against trying to rehash the ultimately innocent action of these farcical comedies:

> BEAUMONT: Fletcher, will you oblige me by explaining?
> UNCLE JOHN *(coming between them and taking each of their arms):* Suppose we none of us explain anything.[28]

Thus, instead of the careful and logical untying of the other well-made genres, the Gordian knots of the farcical comedies are summarily and quickly cut.

In the mid-century one-acts, the brevity of the farces compensated for the illogic of all the coincidental complications. These longer farces used the pace of action and the speed of playing to compensate for the absurdity of the incidents. Brief, in effect, became quick. Often the truncating of time by speed was written carefully into the plot. Beaumont, for example, saw the alleviation of his troubles with the nearing departure of a train. "We must keep up the devious deception," he cries out, "till he leaves by the forty-five past nine. *(looks at watch)* The fatal—I mean joyful hour approaches" (III-36).

Sometimes the farce writers of this period went so far as to warn prospective producers about the time factor in the text of the published script, such as Lankester's Act III exhortation in *The Guv'nor:* "(N.B.—This Act must be played rapidly.)" (III-34).

The three-act structure with its more complicated action provides the opportunity to expand the function of the characters in one of two ways. First, a relatively small number of characters can be made more complex—that is, given more differentiating traits such as the eccentric characters in Gilbert's *Tom Cobb* and *Engaged.* The alternative is to expand substantially the number of generally undifferentiated characters. Because of the complete domination of action in the French-style farcical comedies, the playwrights invariably opted for the latter plan. The average number of characters in afterpiece farce was six. In the full-length versions of this period the characters numbered from a relative low of ten characters for a farce like Byron's *New Brooms* (1881) to a high of twenty-three characters in Burnand's *The Manager* (1882).

Such large casts required skillful maneuvering and integration into the framework of an intrigue based on complicated misunderstanding: a misunderstanding on the structural level of character is a mistaken identity, a device that is part and parcel of almost every farce of this period. In the afterpiece farces, mistaken identity usually took place between only two characters, such as that between the brothers Box and Cox. Such a misunderstanding required only one discovery for its clarification. In the farcical comedies, the mistaken identities were usually multiplied by several pairs, adding to the difficulty of resolution. In *The Guv'nor,* for example, there are no fewer than five mistaken identities.

Because of their extremely undifferentiated make-up, the characters of the farcical comedies, like those of the mid-century one-acts, were basically stereotypes: older jealous husbands; younger faithful wives; handsome, virtuous, somewhat playful adolescents; old curmudgeons or generous and kind uncles and aunts; society dowagers; annoying in-laws; pesky servants; dim-witted policemen and other public employees. The leading roles were hardly ever characterized physically, except by age. Everyone was assumed to look at least all right, if not attractive, though characters were sometimes given certain infirmities such as obesity, near-sightedness, deafness, stuttering, or forgetfulness. Character traits never got more complex than jealousy, virtuousness, politeness, rudeness, miserliness, generosity, etc. Also, as in the one-acts, the names of the secondary characters in the farcical comedies often denoted their caricature: Miss Fitzbattlaxe in *On Bail,* for example, and Puffin, the baker, in *Uncle.* The names of the victims, while not directly referring to stereotype, are almost all multi-syllabic and convey a sense of their foolish nature and middle station in society. Names such as Mr.

Featherstone *(The Snowball),* Mr. Butterscotch *(The Guv'nor),* Mr. Gigglethorpe (Sim's *Flats,* 1881), Mortimer Mumbleford (Joseph's *Confusion,* 1883), and Jonathan Lovibond *(On Bail)* are typical.

As theatre going became more popular with aristocratic audiences, higher-class characters became increasingly evident in the farcical comedies. Gone are the milkmen, washerwomen, tailors, and printers of the one-act farces with their working-class appeal. The characters of the early full-length farces, while not of the nobility, are upwardly mobile members of the mercantile class—bankers, merchants, entrepreneurs, and the like. In fact, class standing is an integral part of the British farcical comedies. Upward ambition is a general concern of most of the characters.

Victorianism also dictated that it would be improper for women to fill the definitive function of farcical victim. By the same token, Victorian morality was probably responsible for the fact that there are many more integral uncle/aunt-nephew/niece relationships in the farcical comedies than there are parent/child relationships. In fact, it is rare to find an early full-length farce in which an adversary relationship exists between a father and a natural son or daughter. This practice undoubtedly is owing in part to the fact that one of the most sacred aspects of Victorianism was the sanctity of the parent-child bond and its attendant stricture to "honour thy father and thy mother." To treat the relationship with the frivolity of farce would have been intolerable. Moreover, such reasoning is supported by the fact that the sentimental comedies of the period such as *Our Boys* and *Comrades* are heavily concerned with the treatment of "honoured parents" (as they are so frequently designated in these plays) by their children. Aunts, and especially uncles, on the other hand, were fair game for deception and equivocation at the hands of their nephews and nieces. In addition, the uncle or aunt more often than not served the purposes of creating mistaken identities by having always been abroad and thus unknown to the nephew except through correspondence and financial support. In view of British colonialism in India during this period, the subcontinent is the usual place of residence of the unknown uncles.[29] From the early farcical comedy, *Uncle,* to the record-breaking *Charley's Aunt* (1892), the conflict between nephews, nieces, and their relatives is a central concern of Victorian farce.

Similarly, there are no actual knaves of the Tony Lumpkin variety in the farcical comedies of this period. The characters are not the idle rich who can afford the leisurely sport of knavery for the fun of it. Clever servants such as the maid, Betsy, partially fulfill a knavish function, but Betsy's trickery, like that of other servants, is rooted in the mercenary ambition of cheating her master out of his money. The major focus of the farcical comedies, therefore, is on the plight of the victim—the stereotypical husband trying desperately to extricate himself from a largely undeserved, confusing predicament of misunderstanding. As Felix Featherstone laments in *The Snowball:* "You little know the agonies I have gone through, and the frightful complications in which I have involved myself" (III-42).

The victims in the farcical comedies followed a definitive pattern of building desperation to near insanity that can be found in virtually all nineteenth-century farces. In the one-acts, the victim, in trying to extricate himself from the predicament, usually resorted to some sort of physically desperate action like disguising himself, hiding in a closet, or jumping out of a window. Such ploys were, of course, retained in the farcical comedies. But to a greater degree, a new evasion more suited to equivocal complications was added—expedient lying. Thus, in *The Snowball* Felix Featherstone, in the grip of horror, unthinkingly lies to his wife when his note to her is picked up by the maid. Similarly, when Beaumont's bachelor-minded uncle suddenly shows up in *Uncle,* Beaumont reflexively lies about his marital status. Stunned, he confides his dilemma to the audience: "Well—a—*(aside)*—now, which would be more awful . . . either way 'madness lies.' Just so. But madness never lied half as much as I shall have to do" (II-19).

As the complications grow in number, the expedient lies escalate to an outrageous level—in effect becoming complications themselves. The feeling is that if the victim would only come clean his plight would end. However, after the lies have accumulated over the course of three acts, the truth seems too incredible an explanation and is never believed. The effect helps to reinforce the idea of the farcical universe in which man is unable, no matter what he does, to control his own fate. Felix Featherstone is undoubtedly aware of this fact as he prepares to admit his mistakes: "I am painfully conscious of the ridiculous improbability of what I am about to tell you, but it is the truth" (III-42).

In fact, Felix's declaration of the truth creates another misunderstanding. It is diagnosed by the other characters as an indication that he has gone insane, thus increasing the emphasis on the irrational desperation of the predicament. There are five references in both *Uncle* and *The Snowball* to the victim's insanity. In *Betsy* there are seven. Furthermore, Lankester became one of the first farceurs of the period to use a now traditional maneuver by which a late-entering character, perceiving the apparent madness about him, decides that he is in an insane asylum. In *The Guv'nor,* MacToddy, a Scotsman who appears for the first time in Act III, reaches this conclusion after observing everyone's strange behavior. "A'm in an asylum," he declares. "I'm shut in wi' a lunatic!" (II-36). In all, there are nine references to insanity in the play. The doubting of the victim's sanity—by himself and those around him—was a definitive aspect of construction that was part and parcel of virtually every late Victorian farce.

Aside from the high level of desperation experienced by the victim, virtually no other deep emotions are felt by the characters. Because of the total sublimation of character to action, they do not have the psychological make-up nor the time to afford much crying, spooning, sorrowing, or romancing. Even the resulting pain of violent knockabout passes in an instant. Thus, the early farcical comedies are determinedly anti-sentimental.

Following the example set by Gilbert in his original farces, writers of adaptations often set up potentially sentimental or emotional situations only to undercut them with something farcical. For example, in the following love scene from *Uncle* between Emily and Fletcher they each undercut the other's heartfelt sentiments:

> EMILY: 'My love!' You presume, with a wife on the premises to call me 'my love!' Why don't you blush to the roots of your hair? No other kind of blush will meet the case.— *(melodramatically)* It must be a blush to the roots of your hair.
> FLETCHER: I assure you I haven't any—any—
> EMILY: Any roots?
> FLETCHER: No. Anything to blush for...
> EMILY: Oh, you couldn't help it. Your behavior is as unaccountable as it is unmanly. You deceive me heartlessly *(half-crying)* and you cooly say 'you—you—c—couldn't help it.' *(sinks in tears on sofa)*
> FLETCHER: Emily—Emily!
> EMILY *(in same tone as before)*: And you don't blush to the roots of your hair. (III-30)

The final manipulation of thought in the French-style farcical comedies involved the sudden clarification of all misunderstandings, the purging of the victim's desperation, and a calming of the audience's suspense. The French-style farcical comedies accomplished this shift in mood in a manner similar to that of the mid-century one-acts: each farce ends with the victim stepping forward to directly address the audience (often in verse) with a simple Victorian homily that includes a pun on the title of the play. It is a way of saying he is really no worse for the wear of his predicament, and neither, incidentally, are the Victorian domestic ideals that the playwright has just given such a rough ride:

> BUTTERSCOTCH: So pass the gloomy clouds of doubt away,
>   And faith renewed foretells a happier day.
> AURELLIA: Beware, my lord, of jealousy. You see
>   To what it might have brought us, but for *me*.
> OLD MACCLESFIELD: He's about her; Lord there never was no fear
>   Cos all along our sailing was so clear.
>   *(to Audience)* My course was definite you understand—
>   I've had to square THE GOVERNOR—YOUR 'and!! (III-48)

The diction in these farcical comedies parallels the basic tradition of British farce dialogue—nonsense language. Yet in contrast with that of the one-acts, the language of the full-length farces is much more like natural conversation. This is owing in part to the fact that there is not nearly so much blatant punning as in the afterpiece farces. None of this is to suggest, however, that the pun suddenly disappeared from British farce in this period. The best pun, of course, is a play on both a word and an idea, such as Jellicoe's advice to Mr. Butterscotch, the candy-factory owner of *The Guv'nor.* "You've been jolly lucky in the sweet line, Butterscotch," he declares; "*toffee or not toffee, that is the question; but life isn't all confectionery!*" (I-6).

The most frequently used diction device in the early farcical comedies is recurring dialogue. It is hard to find a full-length farce of the period that does not repeat the speaking of a line or dialogue at regular intervals for humorous effect. All of the characters in *The Snowball* who have sneaked off to see *The Pink Dominos* excuse their curiosity with the following identical sequence of lines:

> UNCLE JOHN: Not that I care about that sort of entertainment—
> HARRY: Oh, dear, no!
> UNCLE JOHN: But just to see—
> BOTH: If it *was* really—
> UNCLE JOHN: Precisely so. (I-13)

The calculated spacing and the variant readings by actors of such recurring dialogue is what allows it to be funnier each time it is said, rather than boring or redundant.

The most precise manipulation of farcical language in these plays was required for that dialogue which resulted in misunderstandings among the characters and a simultaneous understanding in the audience—the equivoque. Of course, the use of the equivocally simple "I know all!" was widely used in this regard. A more flexible irony device for accomplishing the same kind of misunderstanding is the aside. Whether the aside was used by the character to talk directly to the audience or simply to speak his thoughts out loud, it was a perfect vehicle for stating the truth or misinformation without any other character hearing. Usually used one at a time, the cleverest farceurs often strung asides together in a parallel, equivocal sequence. For instance, in the letter writing scene from Burnand's *Betsy*, McManus' aside parallels Adolphus's aside in the following ironic manner:

> ADOLPHUS: No, mamma. *(aside)* I must write to Polenta, and postpone the appointment.
> ADOLPHUS *(writing aside):* "Mr. Adolphus Birkett presents his compliments to Madame Polenta."
> McMANUS *(aside, writing):* "Captain McManus presents his complements to Madame Polenta."
> ADOLPHUS: "—and regrets being compelled to postpone the appointment till three o'clock this afternoon."

McMANUS: "—begs to say he has returned to town, and will call for his music lesson this afternoon..."

ADOLPHUS *(directing):* Madame Polenta, 55 Porter Street.

McMANUS: 55 Porter Street, Portman Square.

ADOLPHUS: Portman Square.—I must send it by a hansom.

McMANUS: I must send it from the club. (I-21)

True to the British tradition, farcical comedy humor also derives from nonverbal aspects of voice-produced sounds.[30] In many plays accents, both native and foreign, figure largely. Of foreign accents French remained popular, but Scottish seemed to replace Irish in popularity. Cockney and Yorkshire, on the other hand, were still considered to be the funniest sounding (i.e., lower-class) native dialects.

Funny sounds produced by physical infirmities such as stuttering, snoring, deafness, and lisps also remained popular. In *The Guv'nor* Freddy speaks for a large number of farcical characters when he explains: "I m-meant to! I don't mean a memento, but it's a peculiarity of mine; some extra letters got into my alphabet, and I've n-never shaken 'em off! I've met lots like m'me, though" (I-5).

Even more obviously integrated into the plots of equivocal misunderstanding is the overt physicality of the farcical comedy spectacle. Throughout the entire history of British farce, spectacle was never more important to the overall dramatic structure than in the French-style farcical comedies. At almost every level of construction, spectacle was used to physically illustrate the equivocal misunderstandings, the victim's desperation and predicament, aspects of coincidence, and the ultimate resolution. Incidents of farcical spectacle were also used as substitutes for the most risqué parts of the French originals.

The most crucial use of spectacle in the early farcical comedy plots is as *the* functional element of the inciting incident. Between 1875 and 1884 it is hard to find a farcical comedy in which a misunderstood prop does not figure largely. Thus, the intrigue is set into motion by what is essentially the discovery of anything from a telltale piece of clothing or a misplaced pipe to a baby. Most often, however, it is a simple scrap of paper with some ambiguous, equivocal writing on it. Invariably the reason a character is able to claim that he knows all is because of finding a misplaced note that seems to tell all.

It was Sardou more than anyone else who popularized this "paper" technique. In his plays Sardou consistently emphasized the chance vicissitudes of life as affected by a hand prop or document in arousing suspense. His seminal play in this regard was his famous comedy, *A Scrap of Paper* (1860), in which a lost love letter turns a household upside down. When Sardou was inducted into the French Academy in 1878, the director commented: "The letter! It plays a major part in most of your plots, and every detail of it is vital, container and contents. The envelope, the seal, the wax, the stamp, the postmark, the shade of paper, and the perfume that clings to it."[31]

In an age of pre-telephone communication the letter was perfectly suited as a means of farcical confusion. It can be destroyed, forged, accidentally misplaced, accidentally found, equivocally written, equivocally read, refused to be read, and so on. The device was used so universally in the British farcical comedies of misunderstanding that it would not be inaccurate to call them "scrap of paper farces." In *Uncle,* for example, Emily threatens to expose Fletcher's behavior by using the love letters that he had once written to her. *The Snowball* is set off and rolling, kept rolling, and stopped from rolling by no fewer than seven equivocal notes. Early in the second act, Ethel remarks on the damage that a seemingly innocent scrap of paper has wrought: "Poor old Felix! His little note has cost him a night's rest already" (II-18). Similarly, Adolphus's problem in *Betsy* centers on the maid's possession of his legal promise to marry her written on the back of her photograph.

Overt spectacle is also used to give a concrete aspect to the victim's building desperation. The spectacle device of desperation is the chase, which functions as a unifying device for other traditional *lazzi* such as disguise, concealment, and knockabout. Thus, in the course of his flight, the victim is seen making physically expedient decisions. Accordingly, John D. Hurrell derives universal significance from the farcical chase which he refers to as an "allegorical statement that life goes on and that we get out of difficulty, not by contemplation, but by action—especially ingenious dodging."[32]

The best chases usually build to the end of Act II, culminating in a final stage picture that involves such dodging as window jumping and frantic concealment, as well as fainting, screaming, and dumbfounded transfixion. Such a picture occurs at the end of Act II in *Uncle* as Emily mistakenly concludes that her husband has been unfaithful:

> *(Emily gives a wailing shriek and falls into Uncle's arms. Uncle turns, thunderstruck. Fletcher stands transfixed, and Beaumont, with a slight shriek in imitation of Emily's, collapses into Uncle's other arm. Uncle turns to him, thunderstruck.)* (II-28)

As the final disposition of the characters in the above scene illustrates, these end-of-act pictures help to clarify the status of the victim's predicament. These curtain spectacles accurately demonstrate that a picture is worth a thousand words, for surely it would take a complicated verbal explanation to summarize the extent of two acts of farcical complications.

At the end of Act III the final stage picture of everyone standing in correct marital pairs serves as a visual demonstration that "all" has been revealed to be only a simple misunderstanding; as a consequence domestic bliss has been restored.

The box set, fully accepted after 1870, provided the enclosed space with numerous doors that is necessary to accommodate the concealment and surprise revelations of the farcical comedy chases. The clarification for the audience of exactly where each door leads necessitated the particular attention of the full-length farce writers. In almost every farcical comedy of the period, a speech is inserted in which one of the characters explains exactly what is behind each door. Burnand, a master of the farcical use of doors, has Adolphus give the speech as he tries to direct the hairdresser to a hiding place in *Betsy:*

> ADOLPHUS: Not there, that's the dark closet.*(Hairdresser going to L.U.E.)* That's the way into the street. *(Hairdresser crosses to D.R.2E.)* That's the door leading to the governor's room and the house. My bedroom's there, stupid. *(points to L.2E., Hairdresser exits L.2E. and returns immediately with hand glass)*... That'll do, just brush it a trifle over my forehead. *(knock at R. H. D.)* Come in. (II-22)

Furthermore, the breaking up of the floor space and the decorating of the sets with three-dimensional pieces and props provided logical motivations for a variety of realistic movement. More importantly, these household furnishings fulfilled their well-known banana-peel functions of physically victimizing the farcical protagonist. In his theoretical study, *Tragedy and Comedy,* Walter Kerr analyzes this material function of props in "low" comedy: "Matter," he writes, "intervenes by just being there ... comic man is faced with a behemoth of a material universe, a titanic arrangement of solidities that hem him in as effectively as a maze of mirrors in a fun house. Wherever he walks he bumps his nose."[33]

Of traditional "solidities," hats, costumes, and burning cigars and pipes were used as obstacles in virtually every farce of the period, while blatant business with food became less common. The most frequently used *lazzi* in the early farcical comedies were the various humiliations accomplished with a hat. In our current age of bare heads it is perhaps difficult to appreciate the Victorian propriety of a man's hat, but the sudden, instant foolishness of a hat too large falling over the eyes, a hat too small perching on the crown, or a hat's unexpected contents spilling over the face can be universally recognized. As Birkett observes after putting on the wrong, overly small hat in Betsy: "I always said it [the hat] must come to a head" (II-36). Describing Victorian farce as "madcap" would not be inaccurate.

In the early farcical comedies, costumes often play important equivocal roles in the overall victimization. Misplaced gloves, shawls, capes, and monogrammed handkerchiefs are often misunderstood as indications of scandal as easily as an ambiguously written note. Also, as a means of physically representing the low fortunes of the victim, torn, soiled, removed, and otherwise lacerated clothing is perfect. Accordingly, one of the most common stage directions in full-length Victorian farce is "enters dishevelled."

Of new theatrical objects that became widely used for farcical *lazzi* in these plays, three-dimensional furniture (logically) and newspapers (curiously) figure prominently. Of the furniture, closets and trunks for hiding and chairs for all manner of business are used frequently. Chairs are not only sat upon. They are stood upon; they collapse; they stub toes and shins; they wobble; they are used as weapons (both defensive and offensive); and they are even used as a mode of transportation in a classic bit of business from *The Guv'nor:*

> *(She brings down chair from R., upstage and places it L.C.: both sit; Mrs. Macclesfield sits by Butterscotch's side, L.; he moving his chair away from her now and then during the dialogue; and she following him up.)* (II-28)

Business with newspapers usually involved hiding behind the pages of the sort discussed in Gilbert's *Engaged.* The curious appearance of such business in these farcical comedies undoubtedly is owing in part to the fact that newspapers were just beginning to reach a mass readership in this period. *The Illustrated London News,* calculated to reach a less literate audience than *The Times,* was first published in 1842 and was serving a population of over four million by 1875.[34] Typical of this newspaper business are the three individual bits of concealment that occur in *The Snowball.* The first is a slow-building scene in which an embarrassed Felix Featherstone tries to avoid his Uncle's suspicious gaze during breakfast:

> FELIX *(aside):* He has his eyes on me, I know he has! *(business with paper)*
> *(Uncle during scene pours out coffee and places plate, etc., with his eyes fixed on his newspaper . . . Uncle John proceeds solemnly with his breakfast, every now and then fixing his eyes upon Felix who keeps putting newspaper up and down, first hiding from him, and then looking at him curiously.)* (II-21)

More often than not, such panicked concealment is used by the victim not just to save his reputation, but also to protect his body from punishing farcical violence.

Knockabout is more frequently used in the French-style farcical comedies than in the mid-century one-acts in which the contemporary variety originated. This is owing primarily to the fact that Victorian farceurs found the ever popular knockabout to be a convenient substitute for the more risqué aspects of the French originals. Even though *Bébé,* for example, contains many incidents of running about and hiding, it has nothing to compare with the high level of violence directed against the characters in *Betsy.* For instance, Adolphus and his friend, Dick, come upon their teacher, Dawson:

ADOLPHUS: Oh, you've been a gay old dog in your time. *(nudging him)*
DICK: A slyboots, eh?
(Both dig him in the ribs till he falls, they pick him up, apologizing.) (II-8)

This sort of knockabout, which involves the abuse of one character by another, is of the most common sort of violence found in the early full-length farces. More effective, however, are those incidents in which knockabout is combined with some other farcical device such as the use of properties. In *On Bail* Gilbert used a table in this manner:

ALFRED: How do you propose to treat him?
LOVIBOND *(furiously)*: Treat him! Like this. *(rises and leans over table, and half throttles him, then takes up table and bangs it down. Alfred in great terror.)*[35]

Costumes are often used in a similar manner. In Act III of *The Snowball*, for instance, Featherstone's Uncle catches him by the coattails and whirls him around.

The great emphasis on knockabout, prop business, and chasing in the early farcical comedies obviously required actors with considerable skill at improvisational physical humor. Although the director and the farceur were dictating more and more of the blocking and business to the actors, much of the resulting *lazzi* printed in the published acting editions of the period came from the actors' own invention. That "shtick" which was either too personal to the individual actor or was too intricate or subtle to note down was described simply as "business"—perhaps the most frequently printed stage direction in these acting editions.

Among the major farce actors of the period were Charles Wyndham, who created the role of Lovibond in *On Bail;* Edward Terry, who originated the role of Beaumont in *Uncle;* Alfred Maltby, who achieved fame as Dawson in *Betsy;* and W. J. Hill, who created such outstanding roles as Effingham in *Tom Cobb*, Uncle John in *The Snowball*, and Birkett in *Betsy*. Major farce actressses of the period included Lottie Venne, who was the original Betsy in the play of the same name; Fanny Brough, who originated the role of Penelope in *The Gov'nur;* and Lucy Buckstone, who achieved success with her portrayal of Minnie in *Engaged*. Great farce actors of later years who were making their theatrical debuts in this period include W. S. Penley in 1871, Brandon Thomas in 1879, Herbert Beerbohm Tree in 1878, and Charles Hawtrey in 1881.

The Decline of the French-Style Farce

In 1881 George Sims tried his hand at writing a "New and Original Farcical Comedy" in the style of the French adaptations. The play, *The Gay City*, was not successful; it was universally criticized for its overall poor construction and decidedly slow first and third acts. Most critics were content to let it go at that. Clement Scott, alone, perceived virtue in Sims' failure. He used the occasion of his review to publish a plea for more original farcical comedies. "The reaction," he wrote, "has set in, the tide has turned. Let us hope that its waves will wash the mud and dirt of the French capital from our shores, and that the honest work of our English dramatists will fill our stage and our theatres... Now is the time for our dramatists to come to the front and, unless I am very much mistaken, they will be warmly supported by audiences... who will eagerly welcome our home-made and original productions."[36] Moral indignation aside, Scott pointed out to the would-be, native farceurs that they had put in a considerable apprenticeship working with the well-made form and were experienced in all the standard situations and devices.

The major adaptors were the first to try writing original farces, but like Sims they failed. F. C. Burnand's *The Manager* played to mixed reviews at best. H. J. Byron's "New and Original Farcical Piece," *Auntie* (1882), failed on the basis of its weak plot. Only the good acting prevented its sudden demise. Grundy, the apostle of construction, failed worst of all. His "Entirely New and Original" farcical comedy, *The Glass of Fashion,* which opened at the Globe on September 8, 1883, was savagely criticized on the basis of just those structural criteria which he held so dearly:

> In "The Glass of Fashion" the story is not got on with perhaps for the excellent reason that very little story is contained in the play... Mr. Grundy's story is, in truth, very thin, wizen, and infirm. His characters are most unsympathetic creatures, crudely conceived, insincere, unnatural.[37]

Most likely the difficulty that these writers had constructing a successful, original farcical comedy was owing to their total professionalism at being prolific, successful adaptors. It is, therefore, not surprising that the person who finally succeeded where Grundy, Byron, Sims, and Burnand had failed had no previous experience in writing farce at all.

When Joseph Derrick's "Entirely New and Original Farcical Comedy," *Confusion,* was produced at the Vaudeville on May 17, 1883, Derrick's only previous experience at playwriting was his heavily sentimental "comic drama," *The American* (1882), which had been produced in the provinces. Throughout the rest of his dramatic career he wrote two more moderately successful comedies and only one more farcical comedy, *Curiosity* (1886), that was given a matinee performance at the Vaudeville. Like many successful farce writers of the nineteenth century Derrick became experienced in French-style farce through his career as an actor in many of them that were produced at the Vaudeville. Therefore, Derrick's models for his first farce were the British adaptations—not the French originals. *Confusion* is, in a sense, the ultimate equivocal farce of misunderstanding. In every respect he stuffed the plot to the limit with tightly efficient complications and exploited fully almost every popular farcical device. *Confusion* is an apt title. The plot depicts the standard French-style victimization of a husband whose innocent behavior is misunderstood to be unfaithfulness to his wife. Beyond this, the plot line is practically indescribable. The forty-five major plot complications are magnified by the fact that the *dramatis personae* include not only an uncle (the wife's) but an aunt (the husband's), two servants who are secretly married and whose baby is mistaken for everyone's but theirs, a set of young lovers, a doctor and a plainclothes policeman who are mistaken for each other, and even a little pug dog which is mistaken for the baby and vice versa. Add to this no less than twelve verbal *equivoques* of the "I know all" variety, six equivocal letters, notes, and telegrams, fifteen-odd declarations of insanity—all in the midst of expedient lying, farcical undercuts, consecutive asides, chases and their attendant *lazzi,* double end-of-act pictures of catastrophe, knockabout of all sorts, name jokes, furniture business, door business, and even newspaper business. *The Saturday Review* listed the merits of Derrick's farcical comedy as "briskness, mirthfulness, and ingenuity of construction," as well as "smart and amusing dialogue."[38] Scott, who finally had his successful homegrown farce, was most lavish in his praise:

> The success obtained by the clever play, "Confusion" at the Vaudeville is thoroughly well deserved, and if, as may be assumed, Mr. Joseph Derrick possesses the valuable gift of skill in constructing plays he has a great future before him. "Confusion" is an amusing play, the spirit of the fun is well sustained, and it has the great advantage of not boring people in an age when most playgoers are easily bored.[39]

With *Confusion* the move away from adapting French originals had finally spread to all dramatic genres—so much so, that by the end of 1883, critic Henry Morley wrote:

> The British Drama is no longer written by Frenchmen. It seems as though the English dramatist instead of stealing the Frenchmen's plays ready-made, has rather awakened to the greater advantage of borrowing the Frenchmen's tools and using them to make his own. The recent raising of the general level of the contemporary British drama is due to the adoption of French methods and customs.[40]

The way was finally cleared for the development of a truly native full-length British farce. Ironically, while the new farces would profit from a ten-year apprenticeship with the well-made form, they were not to be in the manner of the former adaptation-style, farcical comedies of confusion and misunderstanding. Joseph Derrick's farce had literally exhausted the possibilities of the equivocal form. At the end of Act II in *Confusion* a character cries out, "Where will all this confusion end?"[41] The answer, as far as the popularity of that particular variety of farce was concerned, was at the end of the run of *Confusion*.

Henry James Byron's death in 1884 accurately symbolized the end of the first period of development of the full-length British farce—a period of development which he along with the likes of Gilbert, Grundy, Burnand, Sims, and Reece did much to initiate and maintain. In effect, they had changed what had been an afterpiece art for over two hundred years into a full-sized major form of drama. In 1885 the Conservative Party theatre reviewer officially declared their accomplishment:

> The fact is both patent and notable that for some time past, the old form of farce has practically disappeared and has given place to the "farcical comedy" (a stupid and contradictory title), occupying three acts instead of one, and forming the staple of an evening's entertainment.[42]

The Golden Age of British Farce was about to begin.

3

The Golden Age of British Farce: 1884–1893

...farce should have as substantial and reasonable a backbone as serious plays.

—Arthur Wing Pinero

By 1884 the full-length farce was a firmly established theatrical fact. Over the next ten years the full-length Victorian farce became England's most popular dramatic genre.

To accommodate this trend, a veritable farce industry was created. In contrast to the previous ten years, the years 1884–1893 witnessed the emergence of playwrights who specialized exclusively in farce, actors who made their reputations performing them, and theatres that made fortunes by producing them. The Criterion, the Comedy, the Globe, the Strand, and especially the Court are known today for their famous farce productions during these years.

Most importantly, the farces of this period differed significantly from the first full-length versions; the French-style, equivoque-dominated, confusion farces of the previous ten years had run their course. It seems that the public's appetite for the formula adaptations diminished as their familiarity with the form finally caught up with that of the critics.

Therefore, to maintain continued audience interest, new farce models were needed. The earliest new sources were adaptations of contemporary German farces—the most influential being those of Gustaf von Moser. In the long run, however, the most enduring and successful model for the farceurs of the mid-eighties and early nineties was a new type of British farce developed by Arthur Wing Pinero.

Two theatrical companies were most influential in the development of these two new forms. Both were ensemble troupes devoted primarily to farce production. Charles H. Hawtrey's troupe at the Comedy Theatre was the primary producer of German adaptations. The success of this theatrical venture was due as much to the brilliant drolleries of its actors as to the plays themselves. On the other hand, Arthur Cecil's and John Clayton's company at the Court Theatre was the major influence in the development of native farce. In addition to skilled actors, Cecil and Clayton depended heavily on the overpowering talent of their resident playwright and England's master-farceur, Arthur Wing Pinero. Taken together, the work of these two theatrical enterprises inspired a new generation of writers to develop new varieties of farcical dramaturgy.

C. H. Hawtrey's *The Private Secretary*

Two farces were especially influential on the playwrights of this period. Just as Albery's *The Pink Dominos* spawned French-style adaptations, so too did Charles Hawtrey's enormously popular *The Private Secretary* (1883) and Arthur Wing Pinero's *The Magistrate* provoke new varieties of Victorian farce.

As one of the first successful attempts to find alternative models, *The Private Secretary* was a very loose adaptation by Hawtrey of Gustaf von Moser's *Der Bibliothekar*—a dark comedy about a stuffy librarian who is mistaken for a young rake. Not only was *The Private Secretary* the first really successful Victorian adaptation of German comedy, it was also the most popular farce ever produced in England up to that time, having played for well over two years before it closed. That the play should achieve such success, and that Hawtrey should be its author seemed most unlikely at the outset.

Charles Hawtrey (1858–1923) made his theatrical debut in 1882 as an actor—not as a playwright. As a light comedian he achieved almost instant success and fame for playing what was euphemistically called a "Hawtrey part," the typical English gentlemen and man-about-town. It was only two years after his first London appearance that he began a long career as an actor-manager with his own production of *The Private Secretary*.

In 1922 Hawtrey was knighted for his life-long contributions to the English theatre. According to Hawtrey, however, he never aspired to such success. Rather, he wrote, "it was thrust upon me."[1] More than any other event in his life, Hawtrey was referring to his production of *The Private Secretary*.

Hawtrey wrote and produced his first version of the von Moser play while at Cambridge at the Theatre Royal in November 1883. Several months later, while he was acting at the Court Theatre in London, Harry Bruce offered to produce *The Private Secretary* at the Prince of Wales' Theatre. The offer, however, was conditional on Hawtrey raising £2000. By investing all that he had and by borrowing heavily, Hawtrey opened *The Private Secretary* at the

Figure 6.   C.H. Hawtrey, 1885
(Illustrated Sporting and Dramatic News)

Prince of Wales' on March 29, 1884, as a "farcical comedy in four acts" with Herbert Beerbohm Tree in the role of the quintessential victim, the Reverend Robert Spalding, and W. J. Hill as the violent Uncle Cattermole.

Despite the presence of such stars, the production appeared to be a failure. The reviews were uniformly disastrous, including that of Hawtrey's close friend, Clement Scott, who wrote of *The Private Secretary:* "It was not very skillfully constructed, nor was the dialogue remarkably brilliant."[2] Even more disastrous were the receipts from the nearly empty houses. After the first four weeks of its run, the play was only grossing about £300 per week. So bleak was the outlook that Bruce posted a closing notice of three weeks at the end of the fourth week.

Hawtrey, on the other hand, did not agree with the theatrical pundits and was determined to save the production by moving it to another theatre on his own. He saw the problems as inherent mainly in the production (in which he had absolutely no input) and not in the play. First, they had hired an untalented, ineffective stage manager. Second, Tree never completely learned his lines. Third, the production included a long unnecessary break between Acts II and III. Finally, and most significantly, the opening four weeks of the run coincided with the period of official mourning over the death of the beloved Prince Leopold. In fact, an examination of the receipts for the closing fifth, sixth, and seventh weeks proved that attendance was growing substantially: each of the final weeks grossed at least £1000.

After securing another personal loan for £1000, Hawtrey took over the lease of the Globe Theatre to which he moved the production of *The Private Secretary* with but a few crucial changes. First, Hawtrey took over the role of Cattermole from Hill. Second, he could not get Tree to come to the Globe, so Hawtrey took what appeared to be a big chance by casting a relative unknown, W. S. Penley, as Spalding. The whole cast, including the new stage manager, thought that no one but Tree, especially not Penley, could do the role. Wrote Hawtrey:

> At the first rehearsal Penley laughed so much when *reading* his lines that Glover was quite upset, and said to me, "Penley will never do for the part if he cannot keep from laughing," to which I replied: "He will be all right. *I* am rather pleased, for it shows that he sees the possibilities of the part."[3]

As it turned out, Penley saw the possibilities of the part so clearly that his performance was universally acknowledged as the major reason for the transferred production's overwhelming success.

Nearly as important, however, were the structural improvements that Hawtrey made in the script. Of all the advice that he received, the most frequent was to compress the play into a more efficient three-act, well-made farcical comedy. Not having any experience in these matters, Hawtrey sought some help from the popular farce actor and dramatist, Cecil Raleigh. Among other suggestions, Raleigh advised him to eliminate most of Act III and put the crucial emphasis in Act II on Spalding (absent previously) by giving him a big entrance. Hawtrey did, and a record breaking run was achieved by finally fitting his fine cast with suitably new—if still somewhat uneven—dramaturgy.

Thus, *The Private Secretary* is unique in that it is unified by a type of structure that was at once new and traditional. This innovative farcical intrigue may be called one of intentional deception. In this type of play, complications in the dramatic action arise from the self-seeking schemes of a character or characters (not the victim), the result of which is the farcical victimization of the undeserving protagonist, who remains blissfully ignorant of the deception until the end. Significantly, complication by the extensive use of overt equivocal misunderstanding, the definitive mainstay of the French-style confusion farces, is not the *modus operandi*. While these farcical comedies appear to be new in comparison to those of the previous period, they have roots extending to the most successful traditions of British farce, from *The Second Shepherd's Play* and *Johan Johan* to *She Stoops to Conquer* and *Box and Cox*.

The subject matter of *The Private Secretary* is also reminiscent of earlier styles in that it is one of the few full-length farces of the late nineteenth century that is not concerned with the predicaments of marriage. Rather it is an upper-class courtship farce in which two nephews attempt expediently to deceive their uncles (and creditors) and only succeed extravagantly in victimizing the undeserving private secretary.

The intentional deception and its results are spread over the course of three acts in a standard well-made pattern with only a few modifications. The play opens with typical farcically efficient exposition as Douglas lamentably soliloquizes about his current predicament.

> DOUGLAS *(L. of table, reading letter):* Of course, uncle's old fad again! It's enough to drive one mad. Any other man would be glad of a fellow living quietly and decently, but he's got the absurd idea into his head that I must sow my wild oats, and will do nothing for me until I've done so.[4]

Douglas's friend, Harry, arrives and also complains of problems with creditors—especially his tailor, the boorish class-climbing, status-seeking Gibson, *and* Douglas, himself, who signed all of Harry's notes. Desperate, and realizing that Douglas will not get any money from his Uncle until he "sows some wild oats," Harry expediently concocts the following deception. He will take Douglas to his proper Uncle Marsland's country estate for a weekend of romantic fun with his pretty young cousin and her friend. They will elude Marsland's puritanical gaze by having Douglas pretend to be the new private secretary, the Reverend Robert Spalding, that Harry was to have hired as a tutor for his cousin. The real Spalding, a shy awkward young man dressed as a parson and horrified by big-city ways, arrives, and the two boys put their scheme into effect. They set out for the country and leave Spalding at Douglas's apartment, hoping that he will be mistaken for Douglas by the creditors.

From this early point in Act I, the complications multiply rapidly, enmeshing Spalding in a tangled predicament of mistaken identity that subjects him to unceasing verbal, mental, and physical abuse. Cattermole arrives from India, and not having seen Douglas in years, mistakes Spalding for him. Outraged at his "nephew's" shy, naive, and conservative nature, he beats Spalding with farcical severity and leaves. Immediately Gibson arrives, momentarily makes the same mistake about Spalding's identity, grabs him, beats him, serves him with a writ, realizes his mistake and the true whereabouts of Douglas and Harry, and asks Spalding for cab fare. Terrified at being in the hands of madmen, Spalding ends Act I by jumping out of a second-story window.

Act II takes place at Mr. Marsland's country estate where the remaining characters are introduced, including Marsland, the young girls, and their eccentric governess, Miss Ashford, who is preoccupied with spiritualism, ghosts, and mediums. As Douglas begins to enjoy sowing his wild oats, everyone arrives: Cattermole at the invitation of his old friend, Marsland; Gibson to collect his payments; and finally, Spalding, looking for his rightful employer. What he finds is a deception desperately out of hand, resulting in a hotbed of mistaken identity, with himself at its humiliating, violent center. Desperately he hides under a cloth, with a shovel for protection, only to be mistaken for a ghost by the girls and thrown into a closet by the boys, who are horrified at his unexpected presence.

Act III continues at the same frantic pace in the form of a desperate hide-and-seek chase as the boys try to conceal Spalding from their respective uncles. Finally, at the late crisis, Spalding's luck is at the lowest ebb when he is mistaken by the uncouth Gibson for a robber, grabbed, and tied to a chair. The obligatory scene consists of everyone entering and identifying Spalding as someone else.

In rapid succession, the summary dénouement proceeds to a quick curtain, although not quite as quickly or summarily as in the French-style farces. This is owing primarily to the requirements of resolving a deception intrigue versus those of an equivocal misunderstanding. Whereas the latter requires merely the simple clarification of a point of confusion, the deception type requires the additional explanation of—and apology for—the deception. Thus, in *The Private Secretary*, Gibson points out Douglas's true identity. Douglas then contritely admits that all was perpetrated so that he could sow his wild oats. In a final reversal, Cattermole is delighted by the explanation and agrees to pay all debts—including wedding expenses. Finally, Spalding's true identity is revealed to no one's greater relief than his own. All of this takes only slightly longer than the mere clarification of identity, but the potential exists within the deception form for longer, more explanatory dénouements.

Overall, the farcical characterizations of *The Private Secretary* reflect certain aspects of class and of the deception intrigue.

The Private Secretary is an upper-class farce. Much is made of the elevated and affluent social status of the characters. Thus, humor is derived from contrasting the acute boorishness of the status-seeking Gibson with the refined Marslands and Cattermoles: in Act II, Gibson is given the opportunity to pretend social sophistication at Marsland's dinner party, but only succeeds in becoming drunk and offensive.

Also derivative of the characters' upper-class standing is the functional presence of the mischievous adolescents (Douglas and Harry). First appearing in eighteenth-century farce, such irresponsible characters had no place in the working-class milieu of the mid-century one-act farce. The mischievous adolescents reappeared occasionally with the advent of the full-length farce in the forms of Cheviot Hill and his paramours in *Engaged,* Adolphus Birkett and Betsy in *Betsy,* and Freddie Butterscotch in *The Guv'nor.* In this vein, Douglas and Harry served as the models that turned a trend into a late nineteenth-century farcical tradition. Hardly a single farce of this period was produced that is not incited into action by the domestic predicaments and deceptions of the rich nieces and nephews of prosperous Victorians.[5]

This overall preoccupation with such deception shifts the focus to eccentric characterizations—a most traditional element of British farce that had not been used successfully since *Engaged.* The result of incorporating eccentrics successfully in farce has always been the rendering of funnier and more memorable characters. In *The Private Secretary* Miss Ashford, Douglas, Cattermole, and Spalding stand out as intriguing creations. Miss Ashford's stereotypical schoolmarmish appearance and attitudes are heightened by her preoccupation with spiritualism, a direct cause of the hysterical chases of Act II.

Douglas is a rarity among British farce characters: his personality undergoes a major change over the course of the play from introspective and conservative to that of rakish young man who enjoys his wild oats.

Cattermole and Spalding also receive special treatments for farce characters of the time since they are actually described briefly but specifically within the text. On the other hand, in the confusion farces it is assumed that the characters are either generally attractive young people or caricatures of more mature types ranging from crotchety to boorish to sophisticated. Cattermole is described on his first entrance as an "old gentleman, loud voice, gruff, short-spoken" (I-19).

Spalding, a "very shy, awkward young man, dressed like a parson, umbrella in one hand, galoshes over his boots" (I-11), is a British original. Along with Dogberry and Fancourt Babberly he is one of the most memorable characters in the annals of farce. His famous entrance business immediately defines the eccentricities of this naive country parson, away from home for the first time:

(Enter Spalding cautiously C from L with goods and chattels, After looking about he comes down to settee, sits, and carefully places his goods and chattels on floor in front of him. After placing props in a row near floats, and box nearest settee, counts them with finger and finds one short. Counts from other end. Considers, realizes he has galoshes on, removes them and satisfied, places hat on top of settee, smoothes hair, handkerchief to nose all before he speaks.) (I-58)

In addition, the very fact that a clergyman is the victim in a farce constitutes a major step over the bounds of previously-held notions of Victorian propriety. Of the major critics Clement Scott was the only one who objected to the spectacle: "Shut, if you choose, as in 'Confusion,' a baby or a dog in a chest, but do not thrust therein a grown-up clergyman, however imbecile."[6] Finally, the overwhelming victimization of Spalding is of the extreme physical variety; he endures more knockabout beating than any other victim in British farce. It is only his timidity, propriety, and ignorance that protect him against the pain.

The deception intrigue somewhat modifies the traditional farcical thought patterns of the characters. The basic deception itself is related to the "happy idea" that unified Aristophanic comedy. But, whereas the Aristophanic schemes always had political or social overtones, in *The Private Secretary* the deception is purely expedient. Furthermore, the deception is originated not by Douglas but by his high-living friend, Harry. It is Harry's happy idea to use his Uncle to deceive Douglas's Uncle Cattermole who, conveniently, has spent the last twenty years in that Victorian haven of farcical ignorance, India.

It is primarily Douglas's responsibility to maintain the deception, but the farcical pressure of rapid complication leads him to increasingly reckless expedient lying—a mainstay device of the earlier full-length farces. Douglas, however, is not the victim of *The Private Secretary*.

Spalding is the true uncomprehending victim of circumstances. His total ignorance of what is happening around him is reinforced by his innocent naiveté of all things urban or sophisticated. True to form, Spalding is uncomprehending to the end. As identities are revealed, Marsland asks Spalding for an explanation:

MARSLAND: But what are you doing here?
SPALDING: Well, by this time I really don't know. (III-85)

The only conclusion he is capable of reaching is the definitively farcical explanation that he is trapped in an insane asylum. In all there are fourteen various disclaimers of insanity in the play.

Befitting its violent nature, the humorous diction of *The Private Secretary* is very sound-oriented. In this vein the most obvious and frequently used diction device is punning. Mostly the puns are very simple and obvious, such as Cattermole's quip: "Well, I've no patience with old women playing patience" (I-21). A few, however, are rather intricately clever, such as the following exchange between Gibson and Cattermole:

> GIBSON: That coat was made by an idiot.
> CATTERMOLE: It was not "made in Egypt." It was made in Calcutta.
> GIBSON: What cutter?
> CATTERMOLE: Calcutta.
> GIBSON: I don't know him! Whoever he is he has made you look an object. (II-57)

There is also a great deal of name joking, the close relative of punning. A great deal of laughter is produced by the recurring mispronunciation by nearly everyone of Cattermole's name, which comes out variously as "Catechism," "Scaffoldpole," "Rattlepole," and so on.

More humorous is the use of recurring diction. All who have a vested interest in keeping the real Spalding concealed order him to stay hidden with the following contradictory warning: "And remember, if you are discovered, you are lost!" When the phrase is first used by Cattermole as he tries to hide Spalding in a chest, Spalding replies:

> SPALDING: Pardon me, if I am discovered I am found.
> CATTERMOLE: Lost!
> SPALDING: Found!
> CATTERMOLE: Lost! *(bangs lid down)*
> SPALDING *(opening lid):* Found!!
> CATTERMOLE: Lost!!! *(bangs lid down)* (II-79)

In addition there is much farcically fashioned whispering, snoring, and hard-of-hearing word play.

Hawtrey used none of the more sophisticated farcical language that was perfected by W. S. Gilbert. Even if Hawtrey had the talent for such writing—which he probably did not—it would have gotten lost amid the extravagant, extreme use of spectacle as the primary element for achieving farcical effect.

In *The Private Secretary* there is almost as much space devoted to describing visual effects as there is to writing dialogue. In the Samuel French acting edition published contemporaneously with the production, nearly forty percent of the printed lines of script are used to describe humorous byplay of the characters. Even though all British farce is to some extent spectacle oriented, there had been nothing like this up to that time—especially in three acts.

This extreme emphasis on spectacle is owing in part to the growing fascination with and use of the new advances in scenic technology. In addition to the universal acceptance of box sets and three-dimensional scenery, the most revolutionary changes had to do with the use of stage lighting. By refining his control over gas lighting, Henry Irving darkened the auditorium at the Lyceum, a practice that gained acceptance in the 1880s. In addition, a new vogue for electrical things included the perfection of the carbon arc spotlight by 1776; in 1881 the Savoy became the first London theatre to switch totally from gas to electric lighting, enabling the creation of more realistic scenic effects.

The Private Secretary was the first major farcical comedy to use the new techniques for humorous effect. For instance, the Act II scene in which Spalding is mistaken for a ghost is made funnier by having it occur in semi-darkness and culminating with a seeming electric shock:

> (*They go upstage. They go up in line on tiptoe holding hands—turn simultaneously. Spalding moans. All start and turn.*)
> EVA (*sees Spalding*): There! There! It's the medium, and it's fast asleep!
> (*Harry advances, touches Spalding, and pretends to be electrified. All start.*) (II-67, 68)

The majority of the visual effects, however, were probably inspired by Hawtrey's experience as an actor and thus derived from traditional sources of *lazzi* and three-act farce conventions. Increased in use to the point of extravagance, these spectacle devices were modified only slightly to conform to the new type of intrigue.

Most conspicuously, the equivocally written note that was a mainstay of misunderstanding in the early farcical comedies is dispensed with entirely in *The Private Secretary*. In fact, the only scrap of paper in Hawtrey's farce is one that Cattermole sets out to pen, but which never gets written. Instead Hawtrey relies primarily upon the visual irony of "entering unobserved" for creating his special variety of intentional ambiguity that characters use for deceptive purposes.

To visually enhance the farcical eccentricities of the characters, business is included that relates to their personal use of costumes and properties. For example, Gibson's attempts at affecting sophisticated behavior continually fail as he never seems to be able to get the hang of upper-class accoutrements:

> GIBSON (*with eye glass*) I wish this glass would stick in (I-7).

What is perhaps the best-known farcical business in the play occurs when Hawtrey pits Cattermole against Spalding in a definitive confrontation of characters. As Cattermole tries desperately to hide Spalding from the others, the following extravagant business is called for, involving doors, props, and costumes:

> CATTERMOLE: Here, I must put you in here for the present. *(dragging to L.I.E. and looking off)* No you can't go in there. *(Swings him around over settee, and takes him up to L.I.E.)* Nor there! *(Ditto to R.V.E. and finally to R.I.E. where he slings him off)* There, don't you dare come out til I call you. Here's a wreck.
>
> SPALDING *(putting his head out):* Would you kindly restore me all my goods and chattels.
>
> CATTERMOLE *(throwing each article separately; gags):* There's your goods *(bag)* There's your chattels *(shawl)* there's your showerstick *(umbrella)* frying pan *(hat)* your Sunday trousers *(parcel)* your tobacco pouch *(galosh)* portmanteau *(band box). (Spalding exits and returns.)*
>
> SPALDING: Pardon me, my periodicals. *(Cattermole hands "Sunday at Home" showing title.)*
>
> CATTERMOLE: There's your War cry. *(Spalding goes, returns.)*
>
> SPALDING: My bottle of milk *(he runs off).*
>
> CATTERMOLE: Third *(throws it. It must be caught off. Spalding returns.)*
>
> SPALDING: Pardon me, my orange.
>
> CATTERMOLE: Play! *(he bowls it. Spalding muffs it and Cattermole kicks him off, saying:)* Butterfingers! (II-60,61)

While most of such business is duly and accurately recorded in the acting edition, some *lazzi* were either so complicated or so variable that they were described in only general improvisational terms, such as *"Business of Spalding and Mrs. Stead of picking up and redropping props to be humoured with audience. Picture at finish of business"* (I-17); or the very intriguing *"Douglas goes C. to Harry in alarm then crosses to top of table for pie business"* (II-40). Obviously, the farcical effectiveness of such intricate byplay was dependent to a great degree on the physical dexterity and pantomimic skills of the actors.

The most notable and frequently used type of spectacle for humorous effect—and the most demanding of the actors' physical talents in this play—is knockabout. *The Private Secretary* is one of the most violent British farces ever written for the stage. The most frequent recipient of the slings and arrows of outrageous farcical misfortune is, of course, Spalding. In the course of the play he is pushed around, beaten, sat on, tripped up, shoved under tables and into chests, tied to a chair, hit with an umbrella, kicked, and starved. The results of Spalding's first encounter with the tempestuous Cattermole are typical of the physical punishment that he is made to endure up to the last moment of the play:

CATTERMOLE: Don't do that! *(Spalding makes for door, L.; and goes off. Cattermole follows, drags him back, and gives him three vicious punches. Spalding squirms and finally falls on floor. Picture.)* How dare you run away when I'm talking to you? *(going round back of table to his seat)* You're a perfect young fiend you are! *(sees blue ribbon in Spalding's coat)* Hello! What's this? *(pointing to ribbon Spalding puts hand up. Cattermole taps it with pen)* No not that! *(pulling coat and hauling him half over table)* What do you want to wear that for now? (I-27)

The ultimate success of all the slapstick in *The Private Secretary* was assured by the brilliant physical talents of the man who replaced Tree to play Spalding, William Sidney Penley (1852-1912). Virtually an unknown when chosen by Hawtrey, Penley had just the right kind of theatrical background for the role. Having made his debut in a one-act farce at the Old Court Theatre in 1871, Penley went on to tour the provinces in comic opera. For several years he played burlesque at the Strand under Mrs. Swanborough. It was *The Private Secretary*, however, that made him a star. So successful was his performance of Spalding that he is usually believed to have originated the part.

According to Hawtrey it was Penley's farcical sensibilities and especially the fact that he was "physically much better suited to the character than Herbert Tree" that gave him greater success with the role.[7] In addition to possessing superior physical dexterity, Penley was simply a funnier-looking person, with a face that one would instantly recognize as a clown's despite the absence of makeup.

When *The Private Secretary* finally closed its two-year run, Hawtrey and his ensemble, which by then included Lottie Venne, tried to duplicate the success of *The Private Secretary* by adapting and performing other Von Moser plays. Their first attempt, *The Pickpocket* (1886), adapted by Hawtrey's brother, George, was unsuccessful. Wrote H. Saville Clarke, "It would be rash to prophesy concerning the career of *The Pickpocket*. It may be said, however, that if it does run, the art of writing a successful play is much easier than some of us have thought it."[8] For the third von Moser effort, Hawtrey hired the master adapter, Sidney Grundy, to do an English version of *Haroun Alraschid*. The result, *The Arabian Nights* (1887), starring Hawtrey, Penley, and Lottie Venne, was a resounding hit.

Other entrepreneurs attempted to capitalize on the popularity of the German adaptations. In 1885, a von Moser adaptation entitled *On Change* by Eweretta Lawrence appeared for a short run at Toole's. At the Strand in 1886 Augustin Daly produced his own version of a Julius Rosen piece called *Nancy and Company*. In 1888 Charles Fawcett's *Katti and the Family Help*, suggested by Meilhac's *Gotte*, was also produced at the Strand. None were as successful as the Globe farces. Despite the presence of the redoubtable Willie Edouin in Fawcett's farce, these productions had neither the experienced ensemble talents of Hawtrey's company nor the dramatic abilities of Sidney Grundy, who, in effect, became the Globe's resident playwright.

The success of *The Private Secretary* proved the theatrical and financial viability of alternatives to the French-style farces of the previous ten years. Models for both a farce of intentional deception and the extreme farce can be derived from Charles Hawtrey's first dramatic effort. *The Private Secretary* was such a popular success that the years 1884–1893 would have undoubtedly been dominated by farcical German adaptations had it not been for a change in the copyright law and the plays of Arthur Wing Pinero. The new law made adaptations less profitable, and Pinero made originality in farce a popular and financial virtue.

Arthur Wing Pinero and *The Magistrate*

It has been difficult through the years to appreciate Arthur Wing Pinero as a major writer of farce because he has traditionally been evaluated almost exclusively as a writer of problem plays and for his influence on the development of a native serious drama. Without denying his seminal influence in this area, it would not be inaccurate to say that Pinero wrote some of the finest British farces ever seen and was the crucial force in the development of an entirely original native form. In addition, Pinero was the first British farceur since Goldsmith to gain an international reputation.

The nature of internationalism in all manner of dramatic writing and production was altered radically in 1887. In that year the Treaty of Berne was signed, finally bringing native and foreign works under the same copyright laws and thus abrogating the old five-year law on adaptations. Augustin Filon considered passage of the new treaty crucial to the independent development of British drama:

> One has to think twice before taking up a piece which is burdened with the necessity of paying two authors; it seems preferable to study our methods, and learn from us, if possible, how to dispense with us. Nothing has contributed so efficaciously, for some years past, to the progress of the native English drama.[9]

Pinero's own influential work in writing original farce was not prompted by the change in copyright law. In fact, the last of his famous Court farces opened concurrently with the signing of the Berne treaty.

Like other great farceurs, Arthur Wing Pinero (1855–1934) had gained an intimate working knowledge of the theatre before he began to write. An enthusiastic playgoer in his teens, he made his debut as a professional actor at the age of nineteen. He spent the next ten years performing with Irving at the Lyceum and the Bancrofts at the Prince of Wales'. Pinero began an early apprenticeship as a writer; when he was twenty-two his first play, a one-act farce called *£200/ Year,* was produced as a benefit. He went on to write five more curtain-raisers before his first full-length play, *The Moneyspinner,* was produced with modest success in 1880. In all he wrote ten plays before his first Court farce was produced.[10] Not one was particularly outstanding or a memorable success, but they were illustrative of the various dramatic influences that shaped his own original style.

Pinero spent the early part of his career as a dramatist adapting French plays, an endeavor from which he learned the craft of well-made structuring. For instance, his second adaptation from the French, *Impudence* (1881), was highly praised for its efficient construction, "as are the many French plays of the same calibre."[11] But Pinero was taken to task for what was his Byron-like mixing of deep emotions and sentiment with farcical incidents. The problem was diagnosed by the critic for *The Graphic* as the creation of characters that are too highly differentiated and too realistically motivated to get caught up in illogical farcical actions:

> Strange things can be tolerated in farcical comedies ... Mr. Pinero has chosen to confound the limits of farce and sentiment, and has asked us to believe, that full-grown people in full possession of their senses are the dupes of absurdities of the grossest kind.[12]

Pinero continued to mix sentiment and farce in unfamiliar ways. In reviewing *Girls and Boys* (1882), *The Times* dubbed his dramatic admixture of tears and laughter "odd."[13] His first work for the Court Theatre was a drama in four acts, *The Rector* (1883). Adapted from a Sardou play, it was universally criticized as being too lengthy. Pinero's first unqualified success, *The Rocket* (1883), was billed as a "new and original comedy." Actually the play was an adapted French farce of the old equivocal style. *The Ironmaster* (1884) was Pinero's last adaptation—perhaps because the play was criticized as too close a translation of the French original.

Pinero's original works prior to *The Magistrate* reflected the influence of two major native sources, W. S. Gilbert and Tom Robertson. Basically Pinero emulated Gilbert's inverted farcical sensibilities and his flair for verbal and visual humor. As for Robertson, Pinero greatly admired his accomplishments in popularizing a new variety of native drama at a time when adaptations from foreign works were all the rage. To Pinero, Robertson was the "craftsman" who almost single-handedly "created a renewal of interest in purely native-born comedy. With the success of his plays at the Prince of Wales' came a demand for goods of home manufacture. The managers sat up and rubbed their eyes and began to think seriously of reframing their policy."[14]

Pinero's first major attempt at originality, *Low Water* (1884), was a total failure. As in the past, the critics objected to Pinero's unabashed mixing of comic and farcical effects. In his evaluation, the critic for *The Saturday Review* took the opportunity to put the contemporary views of comedy and farce carefully into perspective:

> To move to laughter is not the chief, or indeed a necessary, end in comedy.... mirth is complex in expression, and the spirit of buffoonery is uncongenial to the muse of Comedy. Mr. Pinero seems to have forgotten that the ludicrous in art may as easily give offense as provoke laughter;... Throughout the play we have a violent alternation of pathos and farce... where the purest pathos is paramount.[15]

Pinero must have heeded his critics, since his next effort at originality, *In Chancery* (1884), was free of counterproductive effects. A farcical comedy of equivocal misunderstanding concerning a husband who becomes the victim of amnesia, the play is largely free of sentimentality.

Thus, a variety of theatrical influences contributed to Pinero's development as a playwright. His acting career gave him theatrical sensibilities, French drama taught him structure, Gilbert gave him a creative, distinctly British flair for character and humor, and T. W. Robertson inspired him with a nationalistic passion for artistic originality. Finally, his own dramatic apprenticeship of ten plays in half as many years gave him an accurate sense of the affective powers of farce and comedy. He now had the wherewithal to write what was to be his most popular play and one of the greatest British farces of all time.

Pinero's *The Magistrate* was the first British farce to achieve an international reputation since *She Stoops to Conquer*. It opened at the Court Theatre on March 21, 1885, a year almost to the day after *The Private Secretary* premiered and ten years almost to the day after *Tom Cobb*. It did not close until a year later. Since Pinero had written *The Rocket* and *In Chancery* for Edward Terry, it has been assumed that he wrote *The Magistrate* for him also. Actually he wrote the play independently. Meanwhile, the Court Theatre, under the management of John Clayton and Arthur Cecil, experienced severe financial trouble in late 1884 and early 1885 due to the failure of the series of serious plays with which they had begun their season. Pinero suggested that they do his farce, *The Magistrate,* as a total change of pace for the Court. The idea was accepted, and *The Magistrate* was produced with Cecil as the unfortunate victim, Mr. Posket. So successful was *The Magistrate* that it did not even close for the summer holiday. When Cecil went on vacation, he was replaced by Tree, while Mrs. Wood and Mrs. Terry were replaced by the indomitable Lottie Venne and Mrs. Tree. Almost immediately three companies of the play were taken on tour of the provinces and another opened at Daly's in New York. By 1895, *The Magistrate* was being produced in Australia, India, Africa, Germany, Austria, and Prague.

Figure 7.   John Clayton, Actor-Manager of the Court
Theatre, 1887
(Illustrated London News)

When a French adaptation was proposed for Paris, Pinero, perhaps with a sense of artistic retribution, flatly refused.

Those factors that exhibit individuality in form and style in his early plays—such as facility with the well-made play form, the ability to create interesting characters, a flair for eccentricity, and a passion for originality—are all present in *The Magistrate*. Pinero labeled the play "an Original Farce in Three Acts." Pinero thus became the first to apply the term "farce" to the full-length form.

Like *The Private Secretary, The Magistrate* is a farce of intentional deception. Unlike Hawtrey, Pinero did not opt for structural extravagance. Unlike Gilbert's, Pinero's first "farce" was written after a long apprenticeship of eight adaptations and two original works—experience which enabled him to perfect the well-made, three-act structure.

In *The Magistrate* Pinero used the farcically efficient late point of attack along with a standard twenty-four-hour unity of time to efficiently stuff his three-acts with snowballing complications. The initial deception is perpetrated by Mrs. Posket before the action of the play begins: like many Victorian women who objected to revealing their actual ages, she married Mr. Posket, a mild, kind, and exceedingly philanthropic magistrate, and deceived him into believing that she was five years younger than she really was. To complete her story, she has also claimed that the age of her son, Cis Farringdon, by a former marriage as being only fourteen instead of his actual age of nineteen. Cis, precocious even beyond his real age, indulges in all manner of recreations befitting a young playboy—including having a room at the notorious Hôtel des Princes where he gives private suppers for friends. It is to this somewhat questionable establishment that Cis induces his stepfather, Mr. Posket, to accompany him for an evening supper and card games. At the same time Mrs. Posket has learned that Lukyn, an old friend of her husband's (and Cis's godfather), has been invited to dinner at her house. In order to get him to promise not to reveal her son's age she secretly goes to his lodging with her sister, Charlotte. Discovering that he has gone to eat dinner at the Hôtel des Princes she follows him there, where he is dining with his old friend and Charlotte's fiancé, Captain Vale. After hearing Agatha's story and agreeing to keep her secret, Lukyn inadvertently invites the girls to eat with him. They accept and stay so long that the hotel owner frantically announces that they have stayed after legal hours, says the police are on the way up, turns out the lights, and bids them all to hide. In the ensuing confusion Mrs. Posket creeps under a table, where she is joined by her husband, who has unsuspectingly chosen the same hiding place. The police enter and find everyone with the exception of Posket, who was pulled out onto the balcony by Cis, and, crashing through a skylight, escapes with him. Meanwhile, because of Lukyn's strenuous objections to the refusal of the police to set the women free, they are

Figure 8.   Arthur Cecil (Seated) as Mr. Posket in the Original Production of *The Magistrate*, 1885
(*Illustrated London News*)

all thrown in jail. The next morning they are called to appear at the Mulberry Police Court before the local magistrate, Mr. Posket. Dishevelled, distraught, and distempered from being chased by the police all night, Posket confusedly sentences Lukyn, Vale, Charlotte, and his wife to a week in jail. Finally another magistrate, Bullamy, sets matters aright by overturning the convictions on the grounds that the prisoners were all legal guests of Cis, who had properly rented the rooms for the private entertainment of "friends." Identities are revealed, deceptions are admitted, and Cis is to be shipped off to Canada with his newly affianced music teacher, a young girl to whom he had been making fierce love throughout.

The disposition of the intrigue among the three acts is somewhat unique for nineteenth-century British farce. The acts themselves are titled, providing indications of the overall progression from unavoidable deception to ultimate clarification. Act I, "The Skeleton," is taken up almost entirely with exposition as opposed to the traditional method of using an opening summary soliloquy. In a comparatively leisurely sequence of scenes the various characters are introduced. Only after these expository scenes does the inciting incident occur near the end of the act: a letter is delivered telling Agatha of Lukyn's pending arrival. The act ends almost immediately thereafter as everyone sets out for the hotel.

Act II, "It Leaves Its Cupboard," takes place at the Hôtel des Princes where all the characters are drawn into the expected farcical predicaments and confusion—all of which results from the original deception. The action is forwarded by the standard devices of coincidence, time truncation, and concealments culminating in the standard hysterical discoveries, faintings, and sense of farcical disaster.

The last act, like the first, departs somewhat from that of the traditional full-length farcical comedy. Titled "It Crumbles," Act III is divided into two scenes. The first takes place at the police court. Pinero uses this scene to begin a gradual revelation of identities, but cleverly uses them for further complications culminating with Posket's discovery that he has just sentenced his wife, his sister-in-law, her fiancé, and his son's godfather to jail. The second scene, set back at Posket's house, is used entirely as a dénouement almost equal in length to the original exposition. In sequence, Bullamy, Lukyn, and Charlotte explain themselves. Then, in a scene unique in British farce up to that time, Mrs. Posket sits down alone with her husband and, at length, regretfully confesses the truth of her deception, her awareness of his, and then promises never to do it again. A complete explanation of Posket's behavior for the other characters is never provided. To include such tellings would only constitute a repetition of what has been said in private between husband and wife—a breach of Victorian confidence that, viewed on stage, would be unseemly at the least.

By constructing his farcical action more proficiently than Gilbert and by not opting for extreme knockabout like Hawtrey, Pinero had more space and time for careful characterization. So outstanding and unique are the characters of *The Magistrate* that it has often been called a "character farce." Pinero, himself, admitted that he always started writing a play with primarily characters in mind: "The beginning of a play for me is a little world of people. I live with them, get familiar with them, and they tell me the story."[16]

None of this is to say, however, that Pinero's farce characters are on a level of complexity equal to those of the best comedy or serious drama. They were rendered, however, slightly more believable than the usual two-dimensional types by virtue of being assigned more distinguishable physical, social, or psychological traits. Their eccentricities seem all the more conspicuous since they represent deviations, however slight, from the strict dictates of Victorian decorum.

Agatha Posket is a rather new kind of character in British farce. While physically she is the typically attractive young Englishwoman of Victorian farce, she is unusually prominent in forwarding the intrigue. She worked a deception to get married in the first place and starts yet another to cover it up. More significantly, she is a real creature of her time—a farcical incarnation of the so-called "new woman" of the eighties who began to emerge from the shadows of Victorian submissiveness. When advised by her sister to tell her husband the truth, Agatha objects on the novel grounds of losing her position in the marriage:

> CHARLOTTE: Take my advice—tell him the whole story.
> AGATHA: I dare not!
> CHARLOTTE: Why?
> AGATHA: I should have to take such a back seat for the rest of my married life.[17]

Finally, in place of the usual punning ending that embodies some proper Victorian homily, Agatha Posket qualifies the conventional morality of deception farces when she declares that "as long as I live, I'll never deceive you again—except in little things" (III-160).

Cis Farringdon, her son, also seems at first glance to be one of the typical, mischievous adolescents that populate late nineteenth-century farce. His eccentricities are, however, quite original and the source of much humor. First, there is the incongruity of his mature behavior versus his supposed age. Second, in Cis, Pinero has created one of the cleverest, prankish, and distinctly British knaves since Tony Lumpkin—possessing a talent for topsey-turvey logic that he uses to secure his varied pleasures.

> MR. POSKET: Yes, but deceiving your mother!
> CIS: Deceiving the mater would be to tell her a crammer—a thing, I hope, we're both of us much above.

MR. POSKET: Good boy, good boy.

CIS: Concealing the fact that we're going to have a bit of supper at the Hotel des Princes is doing my mother a great kindness, because it would upset her considerably to know of the circumstances. You've been wrong, Guv, but we won't say anything more about that. (I-37)

Aeneas Posket is the third unique eccentric of the play—unlike most Victorian victims he is not plagued by undue jealousy, miserliness, or some other aberration of normal judgment. Like Spalding's, his victimization results from an excess of trust in others and his ignorance of Cis's more entertaining pleasures. Also like Spalding's, Posket's profession is one of respect and dignity never before assaulted by the capriciously malevolent universe of farce. Spalding, however, is characterized almost entirely by a dumbfounded naiveté that serves as an almost supernatural armor against extravagant physical abuse. Posket, on the other hand, is a much more believable victim. A fifty-year-old professional, he is kind, meek, highly respected, and an exceedingly philanthropic husband who is unable to totally comprehend either the liberated attitudes of his younger wife or the libertine ways of his seemingly young stepson. Thus his motives are thoroughly altruistic before they become desperate.

Finally, Posket's ultimate victimization goes beyond the physical punishment of falling through the hotel skylight and being pursued all night through the rain. The humorous spectacle of the all-too-proper magistrate ending up dazedly sentencing his wife, sister-in-law, and house guest to jail for a crime of which he is also guilty constitutes a social victimization unique in British farce.

The thought patterns of *The Magistrate* are consistent with the deception intrigue. Overall, the various deceptions and character coincidences are made possible through the farcical ignorance of being in India. In addition, the truth about Lukyn, Cis, and Vale lies unrevealed on the same subcontinent.

As the various deceptions yield to victimization, desperation builds, causing a general state of expedient lying by Agatha, Cis, Charlotte, and Posket. Posket eventually attains the definitively acute stage of victimization by recognizing his plight ("Everything seems against me . . . Oh, everything is against me!" III-123), and finally by nearly succumbing to a perceived state of farcical insanity (LUGG: "It's my opinion he's got a softening of the brain" III-137). A *deus ex machina* in the form of Bellamy arrives on the scene to overturn the convictions and finally to restore a sense of calm and order.

In *The Magistrate* Pinero finally found a purely farcical method of dealing with the deeper, more serious sentiments—sentiments for which he was criticized for including amidst the laughter of his early plays. The solution was the Gilbertian farcical undercut—that is, the use of a verbal or visual gag to diffuse or make fun of scenes of seemingly honest emotions that include crying, kissing, and heartfelt protestations of love. The reconciliation scene between Charlotte and Vale is a classic example of Pinero's humorous use of the device:

> CHARLOTTE: I couldn't come to you with debts hanging over me. *(crying)* I am too conscientious.
> VALE: By Jove, I've been a brute.
> CHARLOTTE: Y-y-yes.
> VALE: Can you forget I ever wrote that letter?
> CHARLOTTE: That must be a question of time. *(She lays her head on his shoulder and then removes it.)* How damp you are. *(She puts her handkerchief upon his shoulder and replaces her head. She moves his arm gradually up and arranges it round her shoulder.)* (II-90)

Pinero's facility with farcical language is in the sophisticated, native tradition of Gilbert's use of topsey-turvey nonsense, but with his own contemporary refinements. His one-liners, for instance, tend to project a sense of sheer absurdity, such as the brief exchange between the two sisters over Cis's age:

> CHARLOTTE: Oh, come, you haven't quite done that.
> AGATHA: Yes, I have—because, if he lives to be a hundred, he must be buried at ninety-five.
> CHARLOTTE: That's true. (I-26)

And Lukyn, outraged at conventional police tactics, cries "Duty sir, coming from your confounded detective tricks on ladies and gentlemen! How dare you make ladies and gentlemen suspend their breathing till they nearly have apoplexy? Do you know I'm a short necked man, sir?" (II-102).

On the other hand, Pinero used the purely nonverbal aspects of vocal sound for farcical effect more frequently and with greater skill than any other playwright of the period. In the course of the play there is a great deal of funny talking with mouths full of food, screaming, whispering, gasping, and even loud kissing and breathing. In Act I, Pinero uses sound to undercut Posket's romantic inclinations:

> MRS. POSKET: Aeneas! *(He kisses her, then Cis kisses Beatie, loudly; Mr. Posket and Mr. Bullamy both listen, puzzled.)*
> MR. POSKET: Echo?
> MR. BULLAMY: Suppose so! *(He kisses the back of his hand experimentally; Beatie kisses Cis.)*
> MR. BULLAMY: Yes.
> MR. POSKET: Curious. *(To Mr. Bullamy)* Romantic story, isn't it? (I-17)

Pinero's use of spectacle for farcical effect is traditionally standard at best—with only two notable exceptions. Throughout the three acts Pinero employs a selection of favorite British *lazzi* including darkened stage business, concealment, door business, costume business (entering dishevelled), a bit of knockabout, extended food business, hat business, and the well-made curtain spectacles of mass panic and fainting. While sufficiently effective, none of this is particularly inspired.

In two rather unique areas of his stagecraft, however, Pinero does exhibit the type of originality that characterizes the other structural elements of *The Magistrate*. Most conspicuously, he seems to have made an overt gesture at officially eliminating from the stage the *modus operandi* of the old confusion farces—the equivocal scrap of paper. In Act II Charlotte, desperate to talk with her fiancé, summarily rejects written communication in favor of a newfangled electric variety:

> CHARLOTTE: I must speak to him to-night; life is too short for letters.
> A. POSKET: Then he can telegraph.
> CHARLOTTE: Halfpenny a word, and he has nothing but his pay.
> A. POSKET: Very, well, then, Lady Jenkins has a telephone. I'll take you there to tea tomorrow. If he loves you tell him to ring up 1338091.[18]
> CHARLOTTE: You thoughtful angel. (II-86)

Pinero's most portentous innovation in the use of spectacle for farcical effect involves no stagecraft at all. That is, Arthur Wing Pinero was the first major Victorian farceur since Goldsmith to use significant offstage expository spectacle (that which supposedly has occurred offstage). These offstage events inevitably occur between acts and are reported by the suffering characters in long colorful speeches. Invariably these descriptions are of events that would either be impossible or just too expensive to produce on stage. Posket relates his frantic, all-night escape from the police in a breathless soliloquy:

> MR. POSKET: Oh! Cis was all right, because I fell underneath; I felt it was my duty to do so. Then what occurred? A dark room, redolent of onions and cabbages and parafin oil, and Cis dragging me over the stone floor, saying, "We're in the scullery, Guv; let's try and find the tradesmen's door." Next, the night air—oh how refreshing!...Where are we? In Argyle Street. "Look out, Guv, they're after us." Then—then, as Cis remarked when we were getting over the railings of Portman Square—then the fun began. We over into the Square—they after us. Over again into Baker Street. Down Baker Street....On, on heaven knows how or where, till at last no sound of pursuit, no Cis, no breath, and the early Kilbutn' buses starting to town. (III-113)

Perhaps Pinero subconsciously desired to create farcical action and spectacle beyond the limitations of the stage. Such inclinations eventually became common to other original farce writers of the late nineteenth century.

Obviously, expository farce requires an actor with a gift for imaginative storytelling. The Court Theatre had just such an actor in the person of Arthur

Cecil, who played Posket. In its review of *The Magistrate*'s opening, *The Theatre* gave Cecil generally excellent notices, but in particular praised his expository talents: "Mr. Arthur Cecil...was the very perfection of the character. His description of the night's horrors when being chased by the police was inimitable in its mock tragic description."[19]

The overall critical reaction to *The Magistrate* was almost as unique as the play itself. In general, the major critics were unanimous in their lavish praise of Pinero's farce, recognizing the play as a nearly revolutionary British dramatic accomplishment because of its innovative structure. In this vein *The Times* was the most outspoken:

> The French monopoly of farcical intrigue is at last threatened, however, in a quarter where danger could hardly have been looked for. On Saturday evening the hitherto staid and respectable Court Theatre produced an original three act farce by Mr. Pinero entitled [T]he Magistrate which for deftness of construction, ingenuity and genuine fun, equals, if it does not excel any French piece of the kind seen of recent years.... his forte as *The Magistrate* proves is farce, or if the term be preferred farcical comedy.[20]

The play was lauded by *The Saturday Review*, which noted that "in spite of its tendency to extravagance, proper enough to a farce as it avowedly is, natural personages live the life of the day."[21] The critic for *The Athenaeum* wrote that *The Magistrate* is "ingenious in construction and witty in dialogue" and on the whole "profoundly diverting."[22] Clement Scott echoed these opinions by writing that "it is written with a dry humour and quaintness of expression very seldom found in the best plays of the kind."[23]

Despite the accuracy of their perceptions of *The Magistrate*, the comments of these critics display a lack of historical perspective. For instance, to a person, these critics classified as an original, native virtue the fact that *The Magistrate* was a decent play without any of the objectionable features of the Palais-Royal pieces. *The Magistrate*, however, deals substantially with suspicions of unfaithfulness and illicit love affairs—all of which result from the accidental meeting of the various suspects at a hotel restaurant reminiscent of a similar notorious establishment in *The Pink Dominos*. In addition, the victim is a highly respected and decorous individual who is nearly driven mad by a nineteen-year-old playboy who gambles, drinks, smokes, and makes love onstage to two girls at once. Ironically, what constituted the stuff of "a wretched, loathsome history" in 1877 was being viewed as "decent" and "innocent" eight years later. Such was the inevitable liberalization of Victorianism in the last fifteen years of the century. Moreover, the major critics of the day had accorded Pinero's "farce" such unheard-of praise as "ingenious," "genuine fun," "rare cleverness," "a very excellent farce indeed," and "profoundly diverting." Superlative praise of this rank has always been reserved for the great works of art in any age. Even Pinero, himself, could not help agreeing with his critics that he had indeed tried to create something different and important with *The Magistrate:*

> *The Magistrate* is a farce, pure and simple. It is an attempt—and has been cordially received as such by the London press—to raise farce a little from the rather low pantomimic level to which it has lately fallen. I have treated it upon lines as artistic as possible, thinking, as I do, that farce should have as substantial and reasonable a backbone as serious plays.[24]

That a genuine farce revolution had been touched off cannot be denied. The production and overwhelming success in one year of both *The Private Secretary* and *The Magistrate* was as portentous in an historical sense as it was in terms of the immediate considerations of profitable theatrical enterprise.

The Other Court Farces

Like Hawtrey's company, the Court management capitalized on their trend-setting success with *The Magistrate* by commissioning Pinero to write three more farces. In successive years Clayton and Cecil produced Pinero's *The Schoolmistress* (1886) and *Dandy Dick* (1887), neither of which quite achieved the success of *The Magistrate,* but were very popular, nonetheless. Pinero's fourth Court farce, *The Cabinet Minister,* was a relative failure.

Ironically, Pinero achieved progressively diminished success as he continued in his attempts to "raise" the artistic level of farce. This is owing primarily to the fact that he included more and more elements traditionally anathema to farce, such as more offstage spectacle, more highly differentiated characters, comic wit, and more complex and deeper emotions. Therefore, while showing his native colleagues how to write good farce, Pinero also pointed the way towards a contemporary revival of laughing comedy.

When *The Magistrate* closed after a run of one year, Pinero was ready with the second "Farce in Three Acts," *The Schoolmistress,* which opened on March 27, 1886, with Arthur Cecil and Mrs. John Woods again in the leading roles. Most notably, the structural efficiency that characterizes *The Magistrate* contrasts sharply with the overstuffed, illogical nature of *The Schoolmistress.* In *The Schoolmistress* Pinero attempted two basic improvements traditionally outside the realm of farce but within that of comedy. In the first place, Pinero expanded the overall characterizations by increasing the number of characters and their level of differentiation over those of *The Magistrate.* Second, significant portions of *The Schoolmistress* constitute rather neatly veiled dramatic satire of Ibsen's plays. In the hands of a less experienced playwright, such a structural admixture would have been a failure. It was primarily Pinero's masterly manipulation of dialogue and spectacle that saved the play.

The Schoolmistress is a deception farce, but the intrigue is much less effective than that of *The Magistrate*. It is not as linear in terms of escalating cause and effect; even its farcical logic is strained. As in *The Magistrate,* Pinero gives titles to the three acts ("The Mystery," "The Party," and "The Nightmare"), thus creating the impression of well-made efficiency. The plot, however, is rather convoluted and difficult to describe. There are, in effect, three separate deceptions going on simultaneously, involving six characters directly and sixteen indirectly. The first act is concerned almost entirely with scenes of exposition that outline the various deceptions. But the central action is Ibsenesque: Caroline Dyott is the schoolmistress of an elite girls' academy. She has rather impetuously married a bankrupt "swell," the Honorable Vere Queckett, and has come to find him an expensive burden. In order to provide him with the comforts to which he is accustomed, she has secretly accepted an offer to perform the prima-donna role in a new comic opera under the stage name of Constance Delacort. Telling Queckett that she is going to spend the Christmas holiday visiting a clergyman's wife in the country, she leaves him in charge of the school, the few students who are staying over the holiday, and the bills to be paid. From this point, the overlapping and parallel complications begin to multiply at a very quick pace. Queckett first decides to throw a bachelor party at the school. However, when his plan is discovered by Peggy Hesselridge, a clever governess-student, and the other young girls, who had also planned a party, they blackmail Queckett into combining the parties *and* into pretending to be their uncle. Predicaments are complicated by the arrival at the party of not only the secret young husband of one of the girls, but also her father, Admiral Rankling (a friend of Queckett's), who has been away at sea for so many years that he does not recognize his own daughter. Included amidst the hilarity of the party is a riotous dance, a frantic "non-eating" scene, and some unlikely romantic pairings. The calamitous climax occurs when the party is halted by some accidentally touched-off fireworks which set the whole school ablaze. All of the characters, except Queckett, escape through the window with the aid of two absolutely looney firemen. Queckett, who has used the money intended for the building's insurance (shades of *Ghosts*—it had expired the day before) to pay for the party, is finally dragged off by Miss Dyott, who has been called from the theatre and arrives at the scene in the fully-plumed stage dress of an opera queen.

With identities and deceptions revealed, the third act begins with the various deceivers madly trying to hide from the wrath of the deceived. Most of the act, however, is devoted to a long dénouement that is the parallel of the exposition as each predicament is resolved separately and consecutively; the husbands are made to confront and submit to their newly liberated wives. Queckett, seemingly ashamed to be married to an opera singer, is about to go back to his "swell" relatives when Dyott's director arrives *(deus ex machina)* with the morning papers which give Dyott rave reviews. He offers her a length-of-run contract at £50/week—a steady income that expediently changes Queckett's mind about leaving. At the same time, Miss Dyott is ironically grateful that the school burned down, since her new career as Constance Delacort rose from its ashes.

Several critics, like the one who reviewed *The Schoolmistress* for *The Saturday Review,* found the plot to be generally indecipherable: "But *The Schoolmistress* has no story. Were an attempt to be carried out to trace the links which run through the three acts, the reader would be left wondering how it could possibly have come to pass that from the rise to the fall of the curtain audiences laugh."[25]

Surely one of the reasons that the audiences laughed so much is owing to one of Pinero's improvements in the area of characterization. That Pinero intended to create more interesting characters is most obviously indicated by the fact that there are so many major characters in the play and that he wrote more detailed descriptions of them than was provided for the characters in any other farce to date, including *The Private Secretary* and *The Magistrate.* These profiles provide not only a description of physical traits, but indications of psychological makeup as well. Of the major characters, none is left at a merely stereotypical level as are several in *The Magistrate.* For instance, the eccentrically contrasting natures of Admiral and Mrs. Rankling are apparent on their first entrance:

> *(Mrs. Rankling is a thin, weak looking, faded lady, with a plain face and anxious eyes. She is dressed in too many colours, and nothing seems to fit very well. Admiral Rankling is a stout, fine old gentleman with short crisp grey hair and fierce black eyebrows. He appears to be suffering inwardly from intense anger.)* (1-45)[26]

The victim, Queckett, is also a distinctive character.

> *(Vere Queckett enters. He is a fresh, breezy dapper little gentleman of about forty-five, with fair curly hair, a small waxed moustache, and a simple boyish manner. He is dressed in the height of fashion and wears a flower in his coat, and an eyeglass.)* (1-35)

Most fascinating are the "new women" of the play, Peggy Hessleridge and Caroline Dyott. Pinero describes Peggy as follows:

> *(Peggy is a shabbily dressed, untidy girl, with wild hair and inky fingers, her voice is rather shrewish and her actions are jerky: altogether she has the appearance of an otherwise neglected child.)* (1-14)

Peggy is the most mischievous of all the adolescents in the play and the primary instigator of the most victimizing incidents. As such, she qualifies as one of the most active female knaves in British dramatic history.

Similarly, Caroline Dyott is one of the most enigmatic, intriguing characters in British farce. Like Nora in *A Doll's House* she has been secretly supporting her husband. Her motive in marrying Queckett in the first place, while class conscious, is at the same time farcically quirkish and expedient:

> MISS DYOTT: I am married secretly-secretly, because my husband could never face the world of fashion as the consort of the proprietress of a scholastic establishment. You will gather from this that my husband is a gentleman. It had been a long-cherished ambition with me, if ever I married, to wed no one but a gentleman. I do not mean a gentleman in a mere parliamentary sense—I mean a man of birth, blood, and breeding. (I-30)

Dyott's most entertaining eccentricity is, of course, her double identity. On the surface Miss Dyott is pure stereotype: "She is a good looking dark woman of dignified presence and rigid demeanor, her dress and manner being those of the typical schoolmistress" (I-26). Underneath, however, lives the flamboyant, comically talented opera singer, Constance Delacort. The final emergence of this vibrant, independent, firm-willed alter ego constitutes the kind of major character change that is rarely seen in Victorian farce.

In the final analysis, however, Dyott-Delacort is more of a structural liability for *The Schoolmistress* than the distinct advantage that the character might appear to be. Although she is potentially the most interesting character in the farce and is the title character, Dyott is not the victim. In fact, she only appears on stage at the beginning of Act I and at the ends of Act II and III. It seems that Pinero might have made a better comedy about Caroline Dyott than a farce about Vere Queckett.

In addition to what amounts to a somewhat comic treatment of the male-female relationship, the typical farcical portrayal of the parent-child relationship is modified. In *The Schoolmistress* Dinah Rankling directly disobeys her father's demand for an arranged marriage by secretly wedding Reginald. This situation, however, is dramatically ironic in an Ibsenesque manner: for all of his objections to what Dinah has done, Rankling's own marriage to Mrs. Rankling was a marriage of love, thus proving—however farcically—that the sins of the fathers are indeed visited upon their children. Moreover, Rankling had been stationed in Malta over the previous four years, resulting in his inability to recognize his own daughter—hardly the picture of an honored parent.

As for the minor characters, Pinero invested even these virtual stereotypes with a sense of eccentricity that borders on the outright absurd. Truly unforgettable in *The Schoolmistress* is the brigademan, Goff—the fanciful madcap ancestor of Ionesco's fireman in *The Bald Soprano*. His particular talent, as explained by his partner, is storytelling. During his one short scene at the end of Act II, as the school is burning down around the hysterical, panic-stricken partygoers, Goff's partner suggests that he entertain them all with one of his famous stories which, of course, he does:

GOFF: It was in July '79 ladies—my wife had just brought my tea to the Chandos Street Station...(II-124)

The reviewer for *The Times* put it best when he wrote, "Dull, Mr. Pinero never is. When he fails to be witty or dramatic, he is at least bizarre."[27]

The more complex characters of *The Schoolmistress* required more complex motivations than those attendant with stereotypes. For example, over the course of the play Queckett goes through the traditional stages of farcical desperation: from a state of calm to a recognition of his predicament ("I can't help it! I am in the hands of fate" II-99) to the brink of insanity ("Get rid of them soon, or I shall become a gibbering idiot!" II-115). Through it all, however, there is the sense that Queckett is not entirely the innocent victim of circumstance. He did acquiesce, after all, in Dyott's deception to keep their marriage and his identity a secret.

The most distinguishing manipulation of thought is that which occurs in the dénouement and is derived from Pinero's unique female characters. In *The Schoolmistress* Pinero used his untraditional, long dénouement to accommodate reasoning and discussion and not merely the clarification of deceptions and misunderstandings. But, to insure that his discussions remain within the realm of farce and not stray into comedy, Pinero was very careful to undercut each one.

Most startling is the obligatory confrontation that follows between Mrs. Rankling and her husband. In a scene that can only be a farcical parody of the one between Nora and Torvald Helmer in *A Doll's House,* Mrs. Rankling makes her husband sit down to listen to her stand up for her rights—all on the threat of walking out and leaving him. The farcical version of this revolutionary scene has the following structure:

THE DECLARATION:

MRS. RANKLING: After seventeen years of married life, I am going to speak my mind at last (III-159).

THE DEMAND:

MRS. RANKLING: And if a mere sculptor could make your wife an ideal, why shouldn't you try? So, understand me finally, Archibald, I will not be ground down any longer.

THE THREAT:

MRS. RANKLING: Unless some arrangement is arrived at for the happiness of dear Dinah and Mr. Paulover, I shall leave you.

THE ASTONISHED REACTION:

RANKLING: Leave me!...Wantonly desert your home and husband, Emma? (III-160).

THE UNDERCUT:

RANKLING (with emotion): And I don't know where to put my hand upon a necktie! (III-161)

The cleverness of the farcical undercutting is indicative of that which literally saved the production and at which Pinero was a master—farcical language. Scott, like the other critics, could not praise this aspect of *The Schoolmistress* enough: "One would advise no less-experienced author to imitate such a venturesome experiment; or, at all events, not until he can write such a dialogue as is here given us. For the dramatist . . . has embroidered on it such a wealth of witticisms as has rarely been found in one play."[28] Although at a minimum, there is indeed authentic comedy-style wit in *The Schoolmistress*. Queckett's explanation of his expedient lying, for instance, has a humorously sensible rather than a desperately non-sensical tone about it:

> QUECKETT: I am being quick, Rankling. I admit, with all the rapidity of utterance of which I am capable, that my assurances of last night were founded upon an airy basis.
> RANKLING: In plain words—lies, Mr. Queckett.
> QUECKETT: A habit of preparing election manifestos for various members of my family may have impaired a fervent admiration for truth, in which I yield to no man. (III-155)

Still, *The Schoolmistress* is stuffed with all sorts of topsey-turvey reasoning, inverted one-liners, name business, foreign accents, and the rather Gilbertian stream of conscious confusion in the form of Rankling's attempt to determine his daughter's marital status:

> RANKLING: Because, Mr. Queckett, I have your assurance as a gentleman that your brother Tankerville's daughter is married to a charming young fellow of the name of Parkinson. Now I've discovered that Parkinson is really a charming young fellow of the name of Paulover, so that, as Paulover has married my daughter as well as Tankerville's, Paulover must be prosecuted for bigamy, and as you knew that Paulover was Parkinson, and Parkinson Paulover, you connived at the crime, inasmuch as knowing Paulover was Tankerville's daughter's husband you deliberately aided Parkinson in making my child Dinah his wife. But that's not the worst of it! (III-156)

As in *The Magistrate* Pinero seems to have delighted in the farcical use of vocal and nonvocal sound. In addition to a breathing-in-the-dark scene almost identical to the one in *The Magistrate* there is the recurring use of mumbling, hubbub and indistinguishable speech for humorous effect. In Act III Reginald, who has been standing outside all night in a raging blizzard, is brought in nearly frozen to death. As the girls attempt to thaw him out, the following not so verbal exchange occurs:

> *(Peggy mixes the grog. Gwendoline and Ermyntrude lead Reginald to a chair before the fire, he uttering some violent but incoherent exclamations.)*
> ERMYNTRUDE: He's annoyed with Admiral Rankling. *(The girls chafe his hands while he still mutters, with his eye rolling.)*
> PEGGY: It's a good job his language is frozen. (III-139)

Also there is a fair amount of screaming and gasping, coupled with such non-vocal, traditionally funny sounds as offstage crashing, falling, breaking glass, and popping fireworks.

The Schoolmistress is stuffed with all manner of traditional and original *lazzi*. The result is a more effective use of laughter-producing spectacle in *The Schoolmistress* than in *The Magistrate*. First, visual effects are used repeatedly to undercut serious emotions. For example, all through the famous discussion scene between Rankling and his wife, Dyott keeps running on and off frantically chasing after Queckett. The incongruity is disarmingly funny.

Second, Pinero worked clever variations on traditional farcical comedy *lazzi*. Act II, for instance, contains a hilarious non-eating scene in which the party refreshments are served, but not eaten; everyone mistakenly assumes there is not enough food to go around. The humor arises out of the entertaining excuses and pretenses made by all to avoid having to eat. Costumes are also used very effectively—especially Dyott's "gorgeous dress of an opera bouffe queen with a flaxen wig much disarranged and a crown on one side" (II-127). Reginald enters in Act II in a "deplorable condition": he is all "covered with snow and icicles, his face is white, and his nose red" (III-139).

Finally, Pinero modified the lighting effect that he used briefly in *The Magistrate* to extend over the entire last act of *The Schoolmistress*. The act begins in the almost total darkness of late night, but as the truth slowly comes to light so too does the stage. The play ends with a called-for brilliant sunrise that comes streaming through the window—not entirely unlike the final effect in *Ghosts*.

But again as in *The Magistrate* the most fascinating visual aspect of *The Schoolmistress* is the use of that device which could not have been enhanced by any amount of stage illumination—reported spectacle. In the earlier farce the use of this device was confined to one soliloquy. In *The Schoolmistress* it is used throughout the play, but in smaller incidents. Such reported spectacle, which accounts for nearly all of the play's knockabout, is of the following variety:

> ERMYNTRUDE *(peeking out the door):* Here's Uncle Vere got loose. He has fallen downstairs.

Especially imaginative are the fireworks exploding to set the school on fire and Dyott's frantic race across town in full operatic costume—hanging on to the back of a firewagon.

Luck was surely a factor in the success of *The Schoolmistress*. It ran for 290 consecutive performances—far short of both *The Private Secretary* and *The Magistrate*. But for its time, it was at least a modest hit.

Like all of Pinero's plays, *The Schoolmistress* was a "venturesome experiment." No two of his works are the same. Therefore, as another experiment in "raising" the artistic level of British farce, *The Schoolmistress* must be considered as a kind of unique mixture of not always soluble ingredients. Having fulfilled his purpose of perfecting an original British farce with *The Magistrate,* Pinero moved in another direction. Like Byron, who had added farcical elements to his sentimental comedies, Pinero began to include traditionally comic aspects in his farces.

Dandy Dick, Pinero's third effort for Cecil and Clayton, opened at the Court on January 27, 1887, as another "Original Farce in Three Acts."[29] It was, in fact, another of his so-called "character farces." But the inclusions of comic material in the form of morally differentiated characters, clever verbal wit, and offstage spectacle are much more obvious and pointed and account for the largest proportion of comedy yet seen in a British play labeled as a farce.

Like *The Magistrate* and *The Schoolmistress, Dandy Dick* is a deception farce, but one with stronger moral overtones. The ethical context is accomplished largely through the use of one strong central victim instead of the myriad of eccentrics used in *The Magistrate.* In addition, the professional status and public respectability of the protagonist are raised substantially above that of the genteel schoolmistress and even higher than the philanthropic magistrate.

The Very Reverend Augustin Jedd, D.D., Dean of St. Marvels, is perhaps the most respectable character ever made the victim of a Victorian farce. As the intrigue begins, the Dean finds himself in the predicament of being £1000 short of what is needed to pay for a new church spire. To complicate matters, his two teenage daughters, along with the Dean's eccentric, widowed, horse-breeding jockey of a sister—Georgiana "George" Tidd—have conspired to deceive the Dean by betting £150 on the 10:1 favorite in the upcoming race, Dandy Dick. Publicly, the Dean expresses outrage and indignation towards anyone who would get involved with horse racing. Privately, however, the 10:1 odds on Dandy Dick cause the Dean to recall his own sporting days as a college student. Unable to help himself, he, too, secretly places a bet on Dandy Dick as a means of raising the church spire money. For the most part, this decision leads only to disaster for the Dean: while trying to give the horse some medicine, he is arrested as a saboteur, but not recognized, thrown into jail, and finally rescued by Georgiana and her jockey friends in a wild chase on the way to the trial. Even when Dandy Dick comes in first, the Dean's winnings, to his astonishment, must go to pay his daughter's bills. Order is restored only when "George" offers to pay for the church spire with her winnings.

Augustin Jedd is the least stereotypical victim in Victorian farce. This is a farcical protagonist with a past—an innate gaming sense that, under pressure, emerges to turn the very reverend clergyman into the sporting dean. Thus, the magnitude of the victimization is reduced since the Dean—quite on his own and without prompting—enters into a deception of his own. This "temporary moral aberration," as he refers to it, belongs more to the world of comedy than to that of farce. The Dean himself recognizes the unique nature of his predicament when he protests, "I am the victim of a misfortune only partially merited." The Dean's moral antagonist, "George" Tidd, is another Pinero original. She is aggressive, loud, and spirited like her horses. She wears the racing togs of a male jockey, but this character is no ordinary farcical breeches part; her getup and manner are not part of some desperate disguise—just pure eccentricity:

> THE DEAN: Remember what you are—my sister—a lady!
> GEORGIANA: George Tidd's a man, every inch of her!

The most striking contrast between *Dandy Dick* and the two previous Court farces is the substantial de-emphasis of humor-producing spectacle; it is virtually all of the reported variety. For example, Georgiana's account of the Dean's rescue is typical of the play's reported happenings that would be difficult to stage:

> GEORGIANA: Why, you were the man who hauled Augustin out of the cart by the legs!
> SIR TRISTRAM: Oh, but why mention such trifles?
> GEORGIANA: They're not trifles. And when his cap fell off, it was you—brave fellow that you are—who pulled the horse's nose-bag over my brother's head so that he shouldn't be recognized. (III-146)

In the long history of British drama, it is the resolution of *Dandy Dick* that is most unique. The use of a highly-respected clergyman as the object of three acts of victimization and ridicule necessitated some special moral and dramatic explanation. Whereas traditional farces end with a direct summary gesture at Victorian ethics, Pinero addresses the audiences of *Dandy Dick* with a call to a new standard. In the final scene of the play, with Jedd worried that the reputation of the Deanery has been damaged by all of his sporting escapades and deceit, his sister argues that he, in fact, hasn't been harmed—only harmlessly laughed at:

> GEORGIANA *(slapping the Dean on the back)*: Look here, Augustin, George Tidd will lend you that thousand for the poor, innocent old Spire...on one condition—that you'll admit there's no harm in our laughing at a Sporting Dean.
> SIR TRISTRAM: Why, Jedd, there's no harm in laughter, for those who laugh or those who are laughed at.
> GEORGIANA: Provided always—firstly that it is Folly that is laughed at and not Virtue; secondly that it is our friends who laugh at us *(to the audience)* as we hope that they all will, for our pains. (III-161,162)

With this small passage of dialogue Pinero made what amounts to a declaration that called for the resurrection of humor to ridicule the follies of man—or in other words, laughing comedy.

In view of this revolutionary defense of laughter, it is ironic that *Dandy Dick* was perceived by the 1887 audiences to be not quite as funny as the previous two farces. Undoubtedly the crowds went to The Court expecting to see another harmless Pinero farce full of wild, illogical intrigue and good, original, visual humor. What they got was not necessarily any less—just different and unfamiliar—and in the end, not quite so harmless. In this vein the reviewer for *The Athenaeum* wrote that while *Dandy Dick* contained much that was rollicking fun, "a more cynical piece has rarely been written."[30] In the end *Dandy Dick* was performed 246 times—a run that can only be considered moderately successful by the standards of the period.

The last of the Pinero "farces," *The Cabinet Minister,* opened at the new Court Theatre on April 23, 1890 for a run of 199 performances.[31] As the culmination of Pinero's experimentation with the form, *The Cabinet Minister* is hardly a farce at all—at least not by traditional criteria.

First of all *The Cabinet Minister* was not written strictly for laughs. Throughout there are scenes, incidents, and characters that generate elements of romance, honest sentiment that is not undercut, satire, and even melodrama. Over the course of the four long acts in which the play is written, the effect is often jarring as the action moves from one scene to another. Second, while there is a kind of unique victimization, it is substantially reduced. It is unique in that it involves the first victimization of a woman in Victorian farce. It is reduced in magnitude by the fact that she is entirely the source of the deception, and she is not victimized by capricious farcical circumstance, but by her own vanity as well as by two rather ruthless characters.

Sir Julian Twombley, G.C.M.B., M.P., and Secretary of State, is the cabinet minister, but a very disappointed one. He is anything but rich and is constantly harassed for money. His lot is not much happier, since his wife, to keep up appearances and to launch her son and daughter prosperously in life has gone deeply in debt to the unscrupulous Hon. Mrs. Gaylustre, actually a fashionable milliner, and her unmitigated snob of a brother, Joseph Lebanon. These two force themselves into high society under the aegis of Lady Twombley's introduction, and compel her to get them invited to one of her great relative's houses in Scotland, where they behave boorishly. Eventually Lebanon, through foreclosure threats, induces his victim to steal an official letter describing a canal that is to be constructed in India, so that he may use the information to speculate on the stock exchange. Fortunately, Sir Julian Twombley has been suspicious and manufactures a letter, the contents of which are in direct opposition to the intentions of the government. He informs his wife of this when she is in an agonizingly guilty state of mind and confesses to what she has done. She immediately capitalizes on her knowledge of the truth, wires her stockbroker to buy shares, and thus makes such a fortune that she is able to clear off all her debts, finally settling and securing her domestic situation. The play ends with a wild dancing of the strathspey.

If there is any one effect that is dominant through all of this, it seems to be outright social satire. Thus, the opening exposition, traditionally used in farce to quickly set up an incident that serves to incite a complicated intrigue, is here used to portray Lady Twombley as a product of conflicting social milieus:

> LADY TWOMBLEY: Oh, I'll never forget the fine folks snubbed me and sneered at me when I came to town. Brooke, my son, I declare to goodness that for ten long years I never saw a nose that wasn't turned up! And then pa got his baronetcy, and old Lady Drumdurris gave her forefinger to shake, and that did it . . . when the time came for a few people to like me for my own stupid, rough self I'd got into the way of scattering sovereigns as freely as I used to sprinkle mignonette seed in my little garden at the yale farm.[32]

By the end of the play, however, Lady Twombley joins the ranks of Agatha Posket and Caroline Dyott as a new woman, no longer totally submissive or subservient to her husband.

Sir Julian Twombley's primary function in *The Cabinet Minister* is the dispensing of gently satirical social aphorisms. For instance, when asked by friends about the advisability of a career in politics for their son, Sir Julian replies: "If you attach any trifling importance to veracity as a habit, not politics. If you would care at any time upon any subject to form your own opinions and having formed them, would wish to maintain them, not politics" (II-62).

What little farce-type spectacle there is in *The Cabinet Minister* occurs offstage. Indeed, the only truly farcical element of the play is the characterization of the Macphail of Ballocheevin, a pathetically shy, naive Highland laird of huge stature, vast wealth, few words, and totally under the control of his mother. Interestingly, the part was played originally by Brandon Thomas. His performance was the only aspect of the Court production to receive unanimous praise. In fact, the critics universally panned the play. They all felt that *The Cabinet Minister* was a perplexing and ineffective mixture of genres that added up to anything but a farce.

The critic for *The Saturday Review* seemed most disappointed and speculated that Pinero had failed out of a reckless desire merely to be different:

> Mr. Pinero's new play, The Cabinet Minister, is a curiously nondescript piece of work, alternating between childishness and extravagance, trenching on the limits of drama, comedy, farce, and burlesque entirely without consistent purpose, and only redeemed by witty dialogue and a few incidents, which have the merit of being funny with the demerit of being disconnected.[33]

In farcical terms the incongruity of Pinero's seeming purpose with his labeling of *The Cabinet Minister* as a farce might best be explained as trying to have his pie and throw it too.

Still, the question remains: Why did Pinero label his play as a farce instead of a comedy? Perhaps the answer lies in the fact that *The Cabinet Minister* is not really a comedy by the traditional standards of the time. Sentimentality was still the definitive structural quality of comedy in the late 1880s.

Exemplary of this fact was the most popular comedy of the period—*A Pair of Spectacles* by Sidney Grundy. A loose adaptation of *Les petits oiseaux* by Labiche and Delacour, *A Pair of Spectacles* opened at the Garrick Theatre on February 22, 1890, as "a Comedy in Three Acts." The play is a very traditional nineteenth-century sentimental comedy that is set up as an argument over differing moral viewpoints in which the incorrect, hard-hearted behavior is ridiculed and the cure of "listening to the heart" saves the day.

In *A Pair of Spectacles,* Grundy does his heart warming by reserving tears of joy for proper expressions of sentiment and uses gentle laughter to ridicule unsympathetic folly. Through the symbolic breaking of his own gold-rimmed spectacles, Benjamin Goldfinch borrows his brother's steel-rimmed spectacles and is transformed from a genial, happy, generous, good-hearted person into a cold-hearted being who will not save his best friend from possible ruin. Only when he retrieves his own spectacles is Goldfinch able to see the light, listen to his heart, and return to his old, generous ways. In contrast to *The Cabinet Minister, A Pair of Spectacles* ran for 323 performances and received rave reviews. Wrote Clement Scott:

> If the drama of the present day is to educate and to raise the moral standard of an audience surely "A Pair of Spectacles" will do so, for there is no preacher-preachee. It is deeply interesting and there is in it so much humour as to make one smile and laugh, while leaving its best impression.[34]

In the greater popularity of *A Pair of Spectacles,* however, can be discerned the influence of Arthur Wing Pinero's farces. For laughing in a comedy at human follies—even sentimental ones—is a significant advance over the crying of the previous 150 years.

Early in his career, Pinero had been criticized for being too cynical for an age of sentiment. Pinero, however, ultimately prevailed; the age of sentiment reached its comic peak in 1890. *A Pair of Spectacles* did not start a trend; it ended one.

Thus, in a direct way, the renaissance of laughing comedy was inspired by Pinero's successful farces. His character farces, such as *Dandy Dick* and *The*

Cabinet Minister, with their believable motivations, socially-oriented concerns, and humorous ridicule of harmless follies, demonstrated to George Bernard Shaw, among others, the possibility of using the farcical form to ridicule the harmful follies of man and society.

Pinero was also influential in less polemic ways. *The Magistrate,* with its original English types and topsey-turvey repartee, served as a major inspiration to Oscar Wilde, who called Pinero's revolutionary farce "the best of all modern comedies."[35] Certainly *The Magistrate,* as well as *The Importance of Being Earnest,* the plays of Somerset Maugham, and those of Noel Coward are in the best tradition of the modern, English comic genius.

More pertinent to this study, however, is Pinero's influence on the development of British farce—an aspect of his career as a dramatist that has been almost totally ignored—this in spite of the fact that his farces are his only plays that are consistently revived.

Overall, Pinero's influence on the writing of Victorian farce was far-reaching—from small categorical and structural changes to alterations in the basic British philosophy concerning the form. First, Pinero began a vogue for calling the three-act farcical play a "farce," thus tending to eliminate the rather oxymoronic term, "farcical comedy." Second, Pinero demonstrated the possibilities of working new variations on the old farcical comedy devices that had become so familiar to audiences and critics alike. Pinero's influential innovations were in the areas of clever farcical language, sound effects, and in using new theatrical technology to enhance traditional visual *lazzi.* Third, Pinero popularized the use of the upper-class, institutional, farcical protagonist. Farces with titles such as *The Barrister* (1887), *The Doctor* (1887), *The Deputy Registrar* (1888), *The Solicitor* (1890), and *The Judge* (1890) were frequently produced throughout the last fifteen years of the century.

Finally, Pinero refined and helped to popularize the deception farce. In so doing he capitalized on a general liberalizing trend in society to set his deceptions in the milieu of the harmless follies of respectable men and more independent women. Just how far public attitudes had come in accepting what had formerly been referred to as French cynicism is illustrated by the critical reaction to an 1889 revival of the scandal of the seventies—*The Pink Dominos.* For the occasion, the reviewer for *The Times* waxed philosophical as he reflected on the moral development of farce in the years between the scandalous debut of *The Pink Dominos* and its revival:

By the revival of *The Pink Dominos* at the Comedy Theatre one is enabled to judge of the extent to which during the past twelve years English notions of propriety on the stage have been modified by French influence.... while *The Pink Dominos* will now be seen and enjoyed for its amusing qualities, it will hardly be spoken of with bated breath as a dramatic scandal.[36]

But if the success of Pinero's farces helped to popularize French attitudes, it worked just the opposite effect on the use of French farcical forms. He proved that a native original farce could compete successfully with those adapted from the French or any other foreign source. Indeed, what *The Pink Dominos* did for adaptations, *The Magistrate* did for original British farce: of the farces produced in London between 1884 and 1893, approximately seventy-five percent were original. These figures constitute a more than total reversal of the situation that existed during the previous ten years when approximately two-thirds of the farces produced were adaptations.

If recent scholarship has been slow to credit Pinero with this accomplishment, his contemporaries were not. Of them none was more vocal than Edward A. Morton, who, writing for *The Theatre* in 1887, credited Pinero with touching off a veritable dramatic revolution. "The introduction of the new style of farce, " he wrote, "is the most significant event in the history of the theatre since the days of Robertson":

> For the three whimisical pieces played at the Court Theatre—'The Magistrate,' 'The Schoolmistress,' and 'Dandy Dick' have the heart and the brain of an Englishman in them. To say that the author of these three plays rivals the most expert French dramatists in invention and construction is not to imply a charge of imitation. In manner as in matter, Mr. Pinero's 'farces' are thoroughly English . . . The skill alone with which the characters are individualized raises them above the level of farce and robustious literary talent which Mr. Pinero combines with the dramatic faculty makes these plays an acceptable contribution to the dramatic literature of an age in which dramatists are more numerous than ever and literature more scarce.[37]

Of the original, full-length farces written between 1884 and 1893, most were attempted formula versions of Pinero's Court farces, although some proved to be very popular. Ralph Lumley's *Aunt Jack* (1889), for instance, was written as a vehicle for Mrs. John Wood and produced at the Court during Pinero's hiatus between *Dandy Dick* and *The Cabinet Minister*. Basically the play is a hotel farce similar to *The Magistrate*. With the role of Joan Bryson, Mrs. Wood added another popular, strong-minded, independent female character to her repertoire that already included Agatha Posket, Caroline Dyott, and George Tidd.

Pinero's influence even found its way over to Hawtrey's company at the Comedy Theatre. Having built reputations as brilliant performers of knockabout farce, Penley and company surprised everyone in August of 1888 by producing a well-received, Pinero-style deception farce by W. Lestoq and Walter Everard called *Aunts and Uncles*. Among the other successful, original, Pinero-style farces of the period were R. C. Carton's and Cecil Raleigh's *The Great Pink Pearl* (Strand, 1885), Arthur Law's *The Judge* (Terry's, 1890) and *The Culprits* (Terry's, 1891) and H. A. Kennedy's *The New Wing* (Strand, 1892).

By the time the copyright law was changed in 1887, Pinero's career as a great farceur was virtually over. But he had proven incontrovertably the theatrical viability of original native farces. In so doing he had set his fellow farceurs free from the artistically stagnant trap of foreign adaptations. While some sought only to follow the formula of his success with farce, others used their new freedom to experiment in other structural directions.

The Extreme Farces

Although the Pinero-style deception farces constituted the majority of original British farces produced between 1884 and 1893, the most interesting and successful of the alternative forms were the extreme farces. Alternatively labelled as extravagant or desperate farces this new and original variety derived its basic form from the older, equivocal, confusion farces and drew its inspiration from the extravagant knockabout of *The Private Secretary*. The farces in this category share a common structural feature: some aspect of plot, character, thought, or spectacle is exaggerated to the point of absurdity. In contrast to the relatively believable deception farces, the extravagant variety manipulated logic to its most outrageous limits.

In the extreme farces all of the definitive farcical devices were stuffed into the dramatic action in quantities exceeding anything written or produced up to that time. In general, such farces required the use of more plot complications, a higher level of operative coincidence, more rapidly truncated time, and wilder and more amazing spectacle, all contributing to much higher levels of overall desperation than was usual. The final result was hardly believable, but a lot of fun.

The extreme farces of the late Victorian period fall into three basic categories: object-chase farces, mixed-up marriage farces, and the multiple misunderstanding farces, as well as various combinations of the three varieties.

Object-chase farces were most likely inspired by Gilbert's *The Wedding March*. In this type of farce a seemingly innocent object such as a hat, a note, a dog, or even a baby is inadvertently misplaced, lost, forgotten, or given away by the victim who quickly realizes that the loss is potentially catastrophic—his life depending on its retrieval. Using primarily incredible coincidence, severe time truncation, and old-style "I know all" equivocation, the victim races against all odds and the rest of the *dramatis personae* in a riotous three-act chase to get it back. The predicament is invariably resolved by the discovery that the object was never actually as lost as was thought, nor as crucial to the victim's survival.

One of the first object-chase farces of the post-*Private Secretary* period was T. G. Warren's *Nita's First*, which opened at the Novelty Theatre in March 1884 to excellent notices.[38] In Warren's play the object that is lost and chased is a baby who arrives at the doorstep of the victim, Fred Fizzleton, as he is sneaking home late. A note attached to the child says that it is for him. Afraid of what his wife might think, he decides to get rid of the baby immediately by placing it at a neighbor's front door. No sooner has he deposited the baby at a doorway up the street than a letter arrives from his sister explaining that she has secretly married against her father's wishes, and has therefore asked friends to deliver her new baby to him for a few days. Plunged into the deepest of farcical predicaments, the chase is on as Fizzleton and a host of others madly pursue the baby to an open doorway up the street, to a police station, to an open cab with a sleeping driver, to Scotland Yard, to Edinburgh, three train stations, and finally a workhouse where the baby is retrieved by its real father. Overall, the chase is made up of at least forty-four major complications: sixteen in Act I, twelve in Act II, and sixteen in Act III.

The older style farces from which Warren's play derives its basic working method are recalled by his use of "I know all" equivocation and the thoroughly stereotyped characterizations with caricatured names like Irrascible and Patience Fizzleton, Miss Prim, and Will Frankleigh. Newer trends, however, are evident in the basic intrigue seen in the suggestions of illicit parenthood, the predicaments of a secret marriage, and Fizzleton's late-night, innocent flirtations. Although the relative amounts of such material are small compared to the overall plot, for 1884 it constituted a significant degree of "riskiness."

This mixture of the old and new styles is more apparent in later object-chase farces such as Charles Thomas's *The Paper Chase,* which opened at Toole's Theatre in July 1888. *The Paper Chase* harks back to one of the most basic forms of nineteenth-century farce—the scrap of paper. The twist, however, is that Thomas's scrap of paper is not equivocal in any sense. Rather, it is the object of the chase as the title indicates.

The paper, itself, is nothing more than an old Indian recipe for curry. What makes it so valuable to all of the characters is the fact that as a result of the most farcically incredible circumstances the one who finds the recipe stands to inherit the vast wealth of the Rajah of Boggleypore. Finding it, of course, is the heart of the predicament. The recipe takes the following circuitous path: it is inadvertently given to a young army officer who gives it to a young girl who leaves it on a table from which it is stolen by a servant who hides it in a pile of circulars which are all thrown in a wastebasket from which it is retrieved and used to stuff the lining of a hat which is thrown out of a window only to land on a moving bus where it is found by a person who just happens to be the family attorney from whom the recipe is retrieved only to be grabbed by a senile old man, who, thinking it to be a formula for curing baldness, takes it to a chemist from whom it is finally retrieved attached to a prescription bottle full of curry. Since the recipe is on stage for most of the play, unlike the baby in *Nita's First,* numerous cautions are given by the author to ensure that the crucial paper shuffling remains clear:

(Slips the recipe underneath circulars on table. Note—The circulars should all be white so as to contrast with the recipe which is on blue paper and in a blue envelope—and made up flat and not too thick, so as to admit of their lying easily one on top of the other.)[39]

Such particularity in the placement and movement of props was a prime requisite of most object-chase farces.

Pinero's influence is reflected by a subplot that concerns a young wife, Mrs. Baskerville, a "new woman" who did a little "harmless flirting" while on a recent cruise from India. In the following exchange Mrs. Baskerville defends herself against the accusations of her friend, the very proper Mrs. Pomfret:

MRS. B: Was it not natural that in a time of peril I should cling to him—who had just paid me the greatest compliment a man can pay a women?

MRS. P: An unmarried woman.

MRS. B *(laying her hand appealingly on Mrs. Pomfret's arm):* Don't be hard on me. I have not tastes in common with Mr. Baskerville. I am young, while he is middle-age—can you then wonder that when I met a congenial nature like Captain Kirby's—

MRS. P *(shaking her off. She retreats, L.C.):* Congenial fiddlesticks! Of course Baskerville's a brute—all husbands are—but you ought to make the best of him.[40]

Mrs. Pomfret, however, is soon plunged into her own compromising predicament by the discovery that her husband, whom she had presumed dead years before, turns up alive. Surprisingly, not much is made out of her inadvertent bigamist situation, despite its great potential for laughter-producing complication. It is indicative however, of the second major type of extreme farce.

The mixed-up marriage farces are extravagant variations on the old equivocal farces of mistaken identity. However, instead of involving just one or two pairs of characters in identity dilemmas, this type of farce involves many sets of mixed-up, intricately related characters. In general, the operative farcical devices are disguise and ignorance of identity—usually through extended years of separation. Invariably the intrigue concerns seemingly stable marriages that are disrupted by the return of a spouse long thought deceased, or they are disrupted by some strange, legal technicality that results in the rearrangement of the various married couples. For example, in Ralph Lumley's and Horace Sedger's *The Deputy Registrar* (1888), a costume party is the setting in which four masked men end up marrying the wrong four masked women—all because of their general inebriation and an advanced state of equivocally farcical ignorance of identities. Their predicament is finally resolved—as invariably happens in mixed-up marriage farces—by the discovery that they were never legally married. Conveniently, the term of office of the deputy registrar who had married them had expired the day before he performed the ceremony. As was sometimes the case with extreme farces, the critics found it a bit too complicated to follow. Wrote Percy Fitzgerald: "There was much that was laughable in 'The Deputy Registrar,' and some really clever writing, but the authors complicated their plot too much and spun it out to three acts, making the third one as noisy as it was superfluous."[41]

David Lloyd used another variation on the mixed-up marriage theme in *The Woman Hater* (1887). The victim, Samuel Bundy, is a professed misogynist who inadvertently proposes marriage to—and is accepted by—three different women. He finally marries fiancée #2 and is carted off to an insane asylum. The hilarity is increased when Bundy discovers that the head doctor of the asylum is the father of fiancée #3. In the third act all of Bundy's intendeds, their former lovers, and all of their parents converge at the asylum to drive poor Bundy nearly out of his mind.

Of the playwrights discussed above, only T.G. Warren and Ralph Lumley achieved anything beyond moderate success with their extreme farces. They remain relatively minor playwrights among the hundreds of the nineteenth century. There were, however, two writers of extreme farce who were acknowledged in their own time as masters of the form—although today it is virtually impossible to find mention of their names in any forum, popular or scholarly.

Mark Melford and J. H. Darnley

Mark Melford and J. H. Darnley were among the most prolific writers of original British farce. Each had outstanding humorous sensibilities and a command of the well-made form equal to the most successful farceurs. Of the two, Melford was the most energetic and prolific. Darnley, on the other hand, was the acknowledged master of the form.

Mark Melford wrote and had produced more full-length original farces than any other Victorian playwright. Among a total of more than thirty-nine melodramas, sentimental comedies, and comic operas, fifteen were original farces. It was Melford who popularized the extreme farce. Throughout his career he was criticized for a general lack of style and refinement. But he wrote with such a maniacal energy and command of stagecraft that he was considered to be one of the funniest of all playwrights. In addition, he wrote all manner of extreme farces including mixed-up marriage, object-chase, fantastic spectacle, and combinations thereof.

Turned Up (1886) is typical of Melford's farcical method. It is a classic mixed-up marriage farce that is complicated by the false death and ultimate return of a seafaring husband. A combination of standard stereotypes, at least one unforgettable eccentric, and some of the wildest act-ending spectacle ever, helped to make *Turned Up* one of the most popular plays of the genre.

Three marriages are at stake in *Turned Up*. An eccentric undertaker, one Carraway Bones, has just married the reputed widow of a sea captain. Her son, the young, handsome George Medway, is trying to secure the permission of the very proper, conservative General Baltic to marry his only daughter, Ada. This must be accomplished within twenty-four hours, since the General is about to leave for India. All relationships are severely disrupted by the unexpected and very much alive return of the first husband, Captain Medway, who, in the deliriums of a tropical disease, had married his Negro nurse, Cleopatra, whom he has brought along. In an Act III recap speech, George recounts the whole complicated, absurd predicament to Ada:

> GEORGE: Hear me;—my mother married my father—
> BINA: No!
> ADA: Yes!
> GEORGE: My father goes to sea,—is drowned,—and married again—
> BOTH: Oh, George!
> GEORGE: My second mother is a Kaffir!
> ADA: No, no!
> GEORGE: My first mother marries again, and my second father is a body snatcher!
> BOTH: Oh, horror!
> GEORGE: My first father returns from his watery grave, and brings my niggardly mother with him.
> ADA: George!
> GEORGE: Therefore, in black and white, I have two fathers and two mothers and how *(turning to Ada)* can I ask your father to join in and swell the crowd? Impossible—impossible![42]

All predicaments and complications are resolved, however, when it is discovered that Cleopatra had tricked Captain Medway into thinking they were married. In the end, Captain and Mrs. Medway are reunited, George makes his deadline and marries Ada, and old Carraway Bones pairs off with Cleopatra, whose color, Bones speculates, will be an attention-getting trademark for his business.[43]

The theatrical style of *Turned Up* is very similar to that of *The Private Secretary*. Throughout the play, extravagant spectacle effects are used—especially a great deal of knockabout with Carraway Bones as the Spalding-like victim. In the course of the intrigue he is pushed around, kicked, thrown into a river, clobbered with a shovel, tripped up, and pushed through a window. If there was another famous actor as capable as Penley of playing such violence, Melford had him in the person of Willie Edouin (1846–1908). Together Melford and Edouin developed a working rapport that rivaled that of Grundy and Penley or Pinero and Cecil. *The Times* reviewed their debut project as a major farcical event: "The humor of Mr. Edouin's acting has a character of its own. No recent writer seems to have encompassed this and so successfully as Mr. Mark Melford in *Turned Up*, [which] causes the walls of the Strand Theatre to resound with boisterous laughter."[44]

The most extravagant use of spectacle for farcical effect occurs at the end of Act II in what is probably one of the most complex and most complicated scenic effects in nineteenth-century British farce. The following curtain spectacle occurs on, not offstage:

> GEORGE *(utters a choking cry):* Murder! *(swoons in the arms of Ada. Cleo laughs, Bones falls through the roof of a summer-house, his legs as far as his knees protruding. Nod, who has gone into the summer house to be out of the row, now comes out in a fright, and looks up at the legs of Bones in consternation. Cpt., in his endeavors to conceal his astonishment, knocks away the support and the casement coming down, the Captain's head goes through the pane.)*[45]

In addition to the extravagant use of spectacle, the other definitive aspect of *Turned Up* is the seeming obsession with the extremes of human desperation that take the characters closer than any others in Victorian farce to the borders of outright insanity. Thus, George actually has the police cart away Bones as a rampaging, raving lunatic. In two of his later farces, *Kleptomania* (1888) and *A Screw Loose* (1893), Melford, as the titles suggests, created central characters with real mental aberrations. Melford's preoccupation with insanity found its clearest expression in one of his serious plays. *The Maelstrom* (1892) is a melodramatic version of the mixed-up marriage intrigue, illustrating how closely aligned the two basic forms of farce and melodrama really are. In this play Melford presents an innocent and estimable man who is subject to recurrent attacks of homicidal mania, who marries, not without some double-dealing, a young girl. Eventually the husband is incarcerated and reported dead. The young girl then remarries only to discover that her first husband is alive and repentant. Rather than be caught in a bigamist predicament, the young girl commits suicide. The critics found *The Maelstrom* to be somewhat crude but not without vitality and power.

By 1889, Melford had secured a reputation as a unique writer of farce. In that year he appeared at the Strand in his latest "New and Desperate Farce," *Stop Thief*. Compared to Pinero's Court farces there was absolutely nothing refined about this play, but according to *The Theatre* critic, it was infectiously and unavoidably funny. In this object-chase farce Melford presents one of the most extravagant stage props yet seen:

> Mr. Melford is known as a writer of "extreme" farces. In "Stop Thief" he has surpassed his former productions, and though it was impossible to prevent oneself from laughing at the extravagant situations, one was compelled to feel that one man standing on his head and another rushing across the stage twice without his trousers was neither refined nor artistic. The whole thing turns upon the loss of a pair of inexpressibles.[46]

The fact that *The Theatre* was not outraged by this inexpressible spectacle was one of the most concrete measures yet of the evolution of Victorian propriety since the days of the first farcical comedies.

Unmentionables also figure largely in J. Herbert Darnley's first farce, *The Barrister,* which opened a successful run at the Comedy Theatre on September 6, 1887—just as *Dandy Dick* was about to close. Darnley was a young actor experienced in performing farce when he set out to write the play. He sought the advice of George Manville Fenn, a writer of melodramas, in the area of basic dramatic structuring. The result of their collaboration is indicative of Darnley's unique treatment of extreme farces.

Basically, Darnley took the standard object-chase and mixed-up marriage formulas and combined them into one highly complicated well-made farcical intrigue. Specifically, Darnley worked a variation on the old French-type equivocal confusion farces. In plays like Derrick's *Confusion,* farcical magnitude can be measured by the number of equivocal complications. Darnley, however, constructed his intrigues so that while there were fewer one-to-one misunderstandings, each constituted a multiple equivocation. In other words, several characters would misunderstand the same thing in a different way at the same moment. In order to accomplish such double and triple misunderstandings, Darnley made use of just about every traditional farcical equivoque, from the standard declaration of "knowing all" to mistaken identity and even the ambiguous scrap of paper which Pinero had taken such care to eliminate.

In order to construct the action of a three-act farce in such a manner, Darnley had to be and was a master of well-made plotting. It is, however, easier to describe what Darnley's farces are than to describe clearly what happens in them. The complicated character relationships needed to create a multiple misunderstanding makes plot description difficult. In fact, the description of the extremely equivocal basic predicament of *The Barrister* requires as much space as does the normally brief plot summary of a regular farce.

The original confusion is owing to the farcical double indemnity of two characters who are both named "Arthur." Mr. Arthur Maxwell is a young, handsome barrister who, upon returning home one night, meets with a young lady who has lost her handbag. With an excess of chivalry, Maxwell hails a cab and escorts her to her door. Since Maxwell paid the fare, the lady takes his address so that she may repay the amount. The next morning, to his horror, he discovers that he took her bag instead of his own, which contains all of his papers for a great legal case he is preparing. Her bag contains lady's undergarments. To complicate matters further, the house in which he is living actually belongs to one Captain Arthur Walker, who is away in India. It was Captain Walker's servant, Tom Price, who took advantage of his master's absence to rent it to Maxwell. Unexpectedly, however, Mrs. Maxwell arrives

Figure 9. J.H. Darnley, 1887
(Illustrated Sporting and Dramatic News)

by an earlier train and is mistaken by Price for the other lady. In this way Maxwell's wife mistakenly concludes that her husband is engaged in an affair. At the same moment, Helen Fayre, engaged to the Captain, arrives with some presents for her fiancé, whom she learns is returning from India. The presents, addressed simply to "Arthur," are taken by Mrs. Maxwell as further proof of his infidelity. Since Mrs. Maxwell ambiguously uses no surname in her references to her "Arthur," Helen Fayre is induced to believe that her fiancé is married to Mrs. Maxwell and therefore writes a letter accusing him of unfaithfulness. She fails to address the letter, and although it is intended for Maxwell it falls into the hands of Captain Walker, who in turn concludes that his Helen is cheating on him. In addition, a Major Drayton, who had wanted to marry Miss Foster (the lady in the cab), breaks off their engagement on the suspicion that she had a romantic rendezvous with Maxwell.

The resulting entanglement sends poor Maxwell on a desperate, wild chase to recover the bag that will extricate him from his predicament. This chase is made probable by a more carefully pointed and consistent truncation and manipulation of time than is usual in Victorian farce. There are seven reminders throughout the play that time is running out on Maxwell—starting with his ominous declaration in Act I: "My life, fame, everything hangs on a few hours!"[47] By Act II the crucial time margin has been reduced to minutes. The final Act III recovery of the bag occurs in the last three seconds—as Big Ben counts down the time.

Because of the total emphasis on action in *The Barrister*, the characters are all stereotypical, young, upper-middle-class Victorian ladies and gentlemen without a single eccentricity among them and with nothing but their names to distinguish them from other farce characters of their kind. Only Kitty Drayton seems a bit different by reason of an assertive air that makes her vaguely reminiscent of Caroline Dyott. Still, none of the characters was given the slightest word of description by the author.

The Barrister was a popular hit with both audiences and critics. Cecil Howard dubbed The Comedy Theatre production "a complete success," and reported that on opening night "the whole of the actors were several times called, and the authors had to bow their acknowledgements to one of the heartiest and most genuine expressions of approval that I have heard for some time."[48]

Darnley's second and only other farcical collaboration with Fenn was produced two years later as *The Balloon*, which opened at The Strand on February 2, 1889, and achieved only moderate success. In *The Balloon*, Darnley applied his unique methods to a mixed-up marriage formula.

The victim of this extreme farce is Doctor Glynn, whose "mere flirtation" has him seemingly engaged to two women at the same time. In addition, he is being legally forced into marriage by the fiancée he does not like and is blackmailed by her bigamist drunk of a husband (whom no one but the doctor knows is alive)—all the while believing that he has mistakenly poisoned his future mother-in-law. He tries to extricate himself from this predicament by escaping in a hot air balloon. When he is not heard from, he is given up as dead. He returns, however, only to be pushed to the brink of insanity, since he imagines that he sees the ghost of his mother-in-law. The knots of this extravagant intrigue are finally cut by the police, who catch up with the bigamist blackmailer and his two-timing wife.

Whereas in *The Barrister* Darnley took advantage of the farcical possibilities of a hotel, in *The Balloon* he shifted the scene to a place of equal potential for spectacle high-jinks—a doctor's office which is immediately mistaken for a private insane asylum. In all of his plays, Darnley exhibited a competent facility with most traditional *lazzi*.

Significantly, there is in *The Balloon* at least one major scene of substantial reported spectacle—the use of which seems to be instinctively endemic to stage farceurs with a flair for exploring the limits of their visual imaginations. Thus, in Act III, Dr. Glynn describes a miraculous escape from the balloon that could never be shown on stage:

> GLYNN: I ran out of the house, pursued by the female demon. I heard the cheering of the crowd and there loomed before me Cameron's balloon...The crowd parted right and left, cheering and waving their hats. With a desperate leap I jumped into the car. In an instant it seemed as if the earth had dropped away and I was stationary, gazing over the side at the woman my horror, my curse...With a maniacal shout I rushed on, that woman behind...shouting aloud, for I was free....The land seemed to glide from beneath me—the sea gulls shrieked...the sails of the vessels were golden in the setting sun and then fate said in a whisper that sounded trumpet-like in my ear—"Stay, murderer, stay!" Hours must have passed, for it was dark, and I knew by the lights beneath me, growing larger that I was falling fast. Then, bump! We struck the ground, wish—sh—we were skimming over the tops of corn. Then we rose at a fence—cleared it...Bumped the ground...and I leapt out trying to hold the monster down. There was a tug...a jerk and the balloon was gone, and I left sitting astride a hedge.[49]

For his third farce, *Wanted, A Wife,* Darnley attempted the mixed-up marriage formula again. This time, however, he fell into what should have been an obvious trap—over-complication. It was "so complex," wrote one critic, "that it puts too great a strain on the facilities."[50] *Wanted, A Wife* had a predictably short run.

Two months later Darnley was ready with his fourth farce, *The Solicitor,* which opened at Toole's Theatre on July 5, 1890. Unlike *Wanted, A Wife,* this play is a masterpiece of farcical plotting in the extreme.

Darnley combined elements from all types of late Victorian farce in *The Solicitor.* First, there is one line of action that works through equivocal misunderstanding to victimize a stereotypical husband, the solicitor. Second, there is an intentional deception of the same husband by his Pinero-type, assertive wife who is trying desperately to pay off her secretly incurred debts. Added to these two intrigues is an object-chase and a group of the most intricately related characters yet seen in any play since *Cymbeline*.

Setting all of these various actions into a comprehensible motion required, of course, extensive exposition for which purpose Darnley used almost all of Act I. The exposition takes the rather novel form of reporting extended offstage spectacle.

As Gilbert Brandon, the solicitor, relates it, he was dining one night with a crack regiment. After dinner he accepted a bet that he would not drive a hansom cab. No sooner did he mount the cab than he was hailed by a lady who turned out to be his own wife. He drove her to her destination whereupon he was astonished to see her kissed by a soldier. No sooner had he left his wife when he was hailed by two burglars who made him take them and their loot to Shephard's Bush. It is at that point that he abandoned the cab which he had originally driven off without the owner's permission. The action begins, and Brandon's situation is further complicated by the arrival of the real cab driver's daughter, Mary Kingston, who engages him, of all people, to defend her father who has been arrested on a charge of being in complicity with the burglars. Also, she just happens to be lodging at the same house to which he drove his wife, where he again witnesses an apparent assignation between his wife and the soldier. In reality, Mrs. Brandon is endeavoring to negotiate for the return of her diamonds which were stolen from her as she was on her way to pawn them for money to pay her bills. In the meantime, Colonel Sterndale and Captain Midhurst, an old and a young Lothario, respectively, have been smitten by Mary Kingston's good looks, and so they arrive at the house on the pretense of helping her in her trouble. They are followed, however, and discovered by their wives. From this point, with everyone converging at the same address, the complications go off in seemingly haywire, almost episodic directions at a madcap, breathless pace until a crisis is reached in which everybody who is married determines to get divorced. Subsequently, a rather long dénouement begins as each line of action is resolved separately and in sequence. Mrs. Brandon gets her diamonds back, admits her deception, and apologizes. The cab driver is vindicated by the capture of the burglars, and the mysterious soldier turns out to be Mrs. Brandon's brother, who finally wins the hand of Mary Kingston.

Although the characters in this most extreme of farcical plots are all familiar stereotypes, the way in which they function within the action is unique. First of all, the presence of Mrs. Brandon's brother is melodramatic in nature. He is perhaps the only character in a major nineteenth-century British farce who does not have an ironic relationship with the audience. His identity is kept unrevealed to the end of the play, thus keeping Mrs. Brandon under some less than whimsical suspicion in the audience's mind throughout. Perhaps the presence of Mrs. Brandon's brother necessitated the creation of a second uniquely functioning character—Lieutenant Arlington—who serves as a kind of *farce raissoneur:* he is not instrumental in forwarding any action, and he is the only young person left unpaired in the end. His only function seems to be the undercutting of all the seemingly melodramatic moments. This he does by being present to continually and heartily laugh at the absurdity of the various predicaments that he observes around him.

Unlike *Wanted, A Wife* the intrigues and character relationships of *The Solicitor* were all, amazingly, perfectly comprehensible in its stage presentation. *The Theatre,* which had given such bad notices to the previous play, found *The Solicitor* to be effective, very funny, and even well balanced:

> Improbable beyond any dream of possibility but intensely amusing is this piece—one that sets you laughing from start to finish, and, strange to say, that has a third act which is very nearly as strong and funny as its two preceding ones. Mr. Darnley is consistent. He sets certain characters before you and gets them into all sorts of ridiculous situations, and lets you laugh at them and keeps you laughing so persistently that you do not stop to consider that such things could scarcely happen, and all the fun is harmless.[51]

This last comment is a fitting compliment to the extreme farceurs. It may be said that, as Pinero reduced the form of farce to its border with comedy, the farce writers like Melford and Darnley stuffed and pushed the form to the limits of its bearable and perceivable humorous magnitude.

After eighteen years of continually playing before the public, an original native British farce method had developed, and it gained popularity over not only foreign versions, but over all other genres of drama. The various varieties of full-length farce had been tested to their popular, if not their artistic limits. It only remained for a young actor whose performing career coincided with the Golden Age of British Farce to use his sensibilities, instincts, and a farcical perspective of ten years to write the most popular stage farce of all time.

4

Charley's Aunt
and the Decline of British Farce

I'm Charley's aunt, from Brazil, where the nuts come from.
—Lord Fancourt Babberly

If there is one Victorian farce with which nearly every current playgoer is familiar, it is Brandon Thomas's *Charley's Aunt* (1892). If the success of a play is measured by the number of people who have attended its performance, then *Charley's Aunt* ranks as one of the most successful plays of all time. In historical terms *Charley's Aunt* was the most popular British play of the nineteenth century, having run continuously for 1469 consecutive performances. In one sense this theatrical record served as the final triumph of laughter over sentiment; it eclipsed the 1875–1877 run of Byron's *Our Boys* by nearly six months.

Ironically, the overwhelming success of *Charley's Aunt* did not serve to popularize a new direction in British farce; Brandon Thomas's phenomenal play was the beginning of the rather rapid decline of Victorian farce.

The Making of *Charley's Aunt*

Like all theatrical blockbusters, the circumstances of *Charley's Aunt's* production were propitious. The dramatic year 1892 was not particularly good for farce. By Christmas fifteen new farces had been produced, but not one of them ran for even one-hundred performances. Of the experienced farceurs, only H. A. Kennedy, George Manville Fenn, and George Sims had their new farces produced—all without much success. The only hit of the season seemed to be an extravaganza with farcical overtones by Harry Paulton titled *Niobe, All Smiles,* which opened at the Strand on April 11, 1892. Paulton's "Mythological Comedy in Three Acts" concerns a man who accidentally brings an ancient statue of a beautiful goddess to life and is subsequently driven from expedient lie to expedient lie in order to avoid the wrath of his disbelieving jealous wife. *Niobe* ran for 535 consecutive performances before closing on July 21, 1893.

Unable to find a new farcical key to popularity in the face of such a paucity of new successes, theatre managers fell back on an age-old entrepreneurial remedy—revivals. Still, the revivals of previous farce hits proved no more successful than any others produced in 1892. *The Magistrate* was revived on April 13 at Terry's for only fifty-two performances. *The Private Secretary* was revived at The Comedy on July 4 with Hawtrey and Penley in their original roles. It played for four months, achieving the only run over one-hundred performances for a farce so far that season.

Hawtrey followed *The Private Secretary* with a revival of his other big hit, *The Arabian Nights* (November 5, 1892), with himself, Penley, and Lottie Venne in leading roles. It closed after less than three weeks.

Of the farce veterans involved in these revivals only W. S. Penley had been thinking of striking out in a new direction. Unaccustomed to failure with a form he had helped to popularize ten years earlier, he began, in 1890, to consider going into management himself. In this regard he asked a fellow farce actor and occasional playwright, Brandon Thomas, to write an opening vehicle for him. Their fortuitous collaboration would make them both wealthy.

There was little indication in Brandon Thomas's early life that he was destined for such theatrical fame. He was born in Liverpool on Christmas Day, 1856, of a Lancashire father and Scottish mother. His father was a conservative businessman who viewed the theatre as the road to ruin. When he was twelve, Thomas's family was beset by financial crisis, and he was apprenticed to a shipyard.

He got his first taste of the theatre in amateur theatricals at private school. While working at the shipyard he took to reciting at the Liverpool "Saturday Evenings for the People." As luck would have it, one night the Kendals heard him recite, were impressed, and told Thomas that if he ever decided on a career in the theatre, he should come to London and look them up. When his father died, Thomas borrowed a pound and went off to London to become an actor.

He made his debut at The Court Theatre on April 19, 1877, as Sandy, the Scottish soldier in *The Queen's Shilling*. He then joined the Kendals' company at a salary of £1 per week. He remained with the Kendals until July 1885, playing small parts in the regular seasons and larger roles on tour in the summers. In August 1885 he went on an American tour with Rosina Vokes (1854–1894), gaining great success as a character actor in light comedies and burlesques. Among his subsequent successes were his performances of Sir Geoffrey in the original run of *Our Boys,* The Macphail in *The Cabinet Minister,* Captain Tom Robinson in the long-running one-act burlesque *A Pantomime Rehearsal* (1891) by Cecil Clay, and Claudius in Gilbert's *Rosencrantz and Guildenstern.*

Figure 10. Brandon Thomas
            (Photograph from the Mander and Mitcheson Theatre Collection)

Thomas's first writing was produced in the late 1870s when he performed his own "coon" songs in music halls. His first play, the heavily sentimental *Comrades,* was written in collaboration with B. C. Stephenson and produced at The Court Theatre on December 16, 1882, where it ran for over a year. His first unassisted attempt at playwriting, a one-act sentimental drama titled *The Colour Sergeant,* was produced at the Princess's Theatre on April 26, 1885. In 1888, Thomas's first full-length farce, *A Highland Legacy,* was produced at The Strand. It was Penley's remembrance of this play that fortuitously inspired him to engage Thomas in what was to be the theatrical collaboration of the century.

At their first meeting over the project, Thomas's inspiration for a "Penley part" was immediate. "You've played every character under the sun," he told the man who created the role of the Rev. Robert Spalding, "have you ever thought of playing a woman?"[1] Thomas finished the first draft of *Charley's Aunt* in two months. When he read it to Penley, the actor is said to have laughed so hard that he fell on the floor and lay there helpless. When Penley became free to take a part, he sent the script to various managements, all of whom turned it down. Therefore, Penley and Thomas decided to try out *Charley's Aunt* secretly—away from London where the critics would not be likely to follow.

They chose Bury St. Edmunds in Suffolk for the opening production in which Penley would star and Thomas would direct. Also secured for major roles were Nina Boucicault and A. E. Mathews. With second-hand scenery, *Charley's Aunt* opened in the small town on February 29, 1892. Thomas himself could not attend since he was still contracted at The Court for *A Pantomime Rehearsal.* The opening night audience at the Theatre Royal Bury St. Edmunds was rather small since Penley was largely unknown in the provinces. The manager, in fact, called everyone down to the stalls before the second act. Their response, however, was anything but meager. They were so overwhelmingly enthusiastic, in fact, that Penley immediately wired Thomas, "Your fortune is made."

While Penley was essentially correct, the financial benefits of *Charley's Aunt* were not realized as immediately as Penley seemed to imply. First, there was not a major London theatre that was available for a new production in March of 1892. When The Royalty finally became vacant in December, Penley and Thomas still needed to raise £1000. They investigated every conceivable source without success, including their relatives and even the backer of *A Pantomime Rehearsal.* Finally, a Miss Sheridan, a descendant of the famous eighteenth-century comic playwright, introduced Penley to a business financier who signed a promissory note for the money. Thus The Royalty was secured; it was only discovered much later that the financier was on the verge of bankruptcy. By that time *Charley's Aunt* was paying back twenty shillings on the pound.

Charley's Aunt opened on December 12, 1892, at The Royalty Theatre, Dean Street, Soho to a capacity crowd. The hysterical laughter caused by that night's performance was unlike anything ever seen in the British theatre. It has been said that the fireman laughed so hard that he fell against the bell and rang down the curtain in the middle of Act I. The Duke of Cambridge's stall collapsed beneath him, and he remained on the floor shaking with laughter. It was midnight before the final curtain could ring down after speeches from everyone in the cast.

In its first week *Charley's Aunt* had over £12,000 in advance bookings. By the end of the month, The Royalty Theatre had proved too small, and the play was transferred to the old Globe Theatre in Wych Street, Strand (the site of Penley's original triumph in *The Private Secretary*) where it ran continuously for four years.

Within a year there were seven road companies touring Great Britain. On October 2, 1893, Charles Frohman opened a production of *Charley's Aunt* in New York at The Standard Theatre with Etienne Girardot in the leading role. Before long the play was touring successfully in New Zealand, Australia, South Africa, and Canada. Brandon Thomas's farce was translated for production into practically every major language. In Germany it played as *Charley's Tante*, in France as *La Marraine de Charley*, in Italy as *La Zia di Carlo*, and in Japan as *The Aunt of Hawaii*. Productions followed in Greek, Turkish, Scandinavian, Afrikaans, Gaelic, Zulu, and Esperanto. In one year *Charley's Aunt* played simultaneously in forty-eight separate productions in twenty-two different languages.

The reasons for the unprecedented lasting popularity of *Charley's Aunt* are several. By genre and subject Thomas's farce is in the mainstream of such traditional British hits as *The Merry Wives of Windsor, She Stoops to Conquer, The Private Secretary*, and *The Magistrate*. First, *Charley's Aunt* is thoroughly British in manners and characters with a unique and totally new central victim. Second, the dialogue is brilliantly crafted in farcical patterns. Third, the play is stuffed with intricately hilarious knockabout and an assortment of surefire traditional *lazzi*. Finally, the overall efficient construction of the deception intrigue keeps the laughter building right to the end of its three acts.

Like *The Private Secretary, Charley's Aunt* is one of the few late Victorian farces that is not concerned with the domestic imbroglios of marriage. It is a courtship farce in which Penley once again played an innocent bystander victimized by the amorous deceptions of two young would-be Lotharios. For the record, the basic dramatic action of *Charley's Aunt* is as follows: two young Oxford undergrads, Jack Chesney and Charley Wykeham, are preparing to entertain their sweethearts at a lunch which Charley's elderly aunt, the wealthy Donna Lucia D'Alvadorez (whom Charley has never seen), is to chaperone. Their plans are nearly upset when at the last moment, by the "merest coincidence in the world," the aunt's arrival from Brazil is delayed. Since it would not only be undesirable but absolutely impossible to postpone the affair (since everyone is leaving for a different part of the country in the morning), the two young men expediently concoct a deception with the unwilling help of fellow undergrad Lord Fancourt "Babbs" Babberly, who has coincidentally been cast as an elderly lady in an amateur theatrical. Since Babbs already possesses the necessary costume, Charley and Jack pressure him into masquerading as Charley's aunt—only for the purposes of the scheduled lunch. Hilarious complications quickly ensue, however, as Babbs is romantically pursued by two elderly gentlemen after the widowed aunt's money. Furthermore, the real aunt returns and, to have some fun, withholds her identity and assists in sustaining the deception. Throughout, Babbs is prevented from ending the charade by the coercive knockabout of his two friends and by his own delight in his incognito proximity to the young ladies. The action is resolved when the real Donna Lucia D'Alvadorez reveals her identity, thus enabling everyone including herself to become engaged to their true loves. Finally, as he takes the hand of his sweetheart, Babbs renounces "all claims to 'Charley's Aunt.'"[2]

From beginning to end the intrigue is a classic example of efficient, well-made farcical construction. Thomas used all of the best plot devices, along with a sense of manners and even a touch of sentiment in putting together one of the most efficient farces of the nineteenth century. Act I sets up the predicament and begins the increasingly desperate victimization. The rather long exposition (two-thirds of Act I) needed to set up the predicament is alleviated by jokes, sight gags, and knockabout that builds to a major curtain complication in which the two older men (the miserly, crotchety Spettigue and Jack's father, Sir Francis) make awkwardly romantic advances towards the disguised Babbs.

In Act II new characters are introduced and several seemingly calamitous complications occur. Jack's father proposes to Babbs. At the same time the two girls, Amy and Kitty, accept the marriage proposals of Charley and Jack only to discover that they must obtain Spettigue's written consent, which he is unwilling to give. Finally the real Donna Lucia, along with a young charge (in love with Babbs), arrives. All of the discoveries and reversals of Act II are unified by an act-long chase as Babbs is frantically pursued by Sir Francis, Spettigue, Jack, and Charley.

Act III is Thomas's cleverest construction. In neat form he solved the problem that had plagued writers of three-act farces since 1875: how to construct a third act that sustains and builds on the high level of hilarity that is achieved at the end of Act II without being too noisy. First of all the third act of *Charley's Aunt* is much shorter than is usually found in Victorian farce; in most, the three acts are approximately equal in length. Act III of *Charley's Aunt* is one half the length of each of the previous two.

Second, to relieve the noise and desperation, the scenes of Act III proceed in a sequence of cleverly contrasted tones. The first scene continues the chase from Act II as Charley and Jack grab Babbs and berate him for his dinner behavior. This raucous atmosphere is deflated when Babbs soberly declares his inability to carry on the "ghastly farrago" because of the coincidental arrival of his true love, Ela. This moment is quickly followed by more hilarity as Babbs is trapped with the women in dainty after-dinner conversation while the men are off smoking his beloved cigars. This is followed by Jack's honest explanation of his love for Kitty to his approving father, which is succeeded by a scene of the broadest humor in which Spettigue proposes to Babbs. What follows is a somewhat less boisterous but still farcical interlude in which Babbs is caught smoking by Donna Lucia. Then comes a delicate, sentimental scene between Babbs and Ela which is outlandishly contrasted by a mockingly similar scene between Babbs and Spettigue. And so it goes up to the resolution, which is rendered all the more playful by the fact that Donna Lucia, who could have ended the charade in Act II, has let it all continue—just for fun. In his review of the play's premiere, the critic for *The Saturday Review* took special delight in the novel structuring of this fluctuating third act:

> The fun soon becomes fast and furious; and one is almost relieved by some love-making, both playful and graceful... The third act is the best and briskest of the three, and the interest increases consistently to the very end—a most excellent thing in farce as in other things.[3]

What the critics and the audiences found most delightful, however, was Thomas's most memorable structural innovation: his farcical protagonist. Lord Fancourt Babberly is certainly no ordinary victim. As he says to Sir Francis, "I'm a woman with a history."

Most noticeably, the nature and function of Babbs' masquerade are different from those of most British farcical victims. Usually disguise is employed to avoid detection by taking another's appearance or identity as in *Tom Cobb, Uncle, The Schoolmistress, The Barrister, The Arabian Nights,* and *The Deputy Registrar.* In *Charley's Aunt,* Babbs dresses up as an old woman not for his own expedient purposes, but at the coercive urging of his friends. Thus Babbs' disguise is the direct result of pure, undeserving victimization rather than the consequence of a deceptive nature. In this regard the female impersonation is the pivot of the play and serves as the primary laugh getter; it is more ludicrous than it is fraudulent.

Babbs' spinsterly getup was also a Victorian novelty—an aspect rarely considered by modern audiences. In the long history of British drama the mainstay of farcical and comic disguise had always been the breeches part—that is, a woman who dresses up as a man. This traditional favorite figures largely in such Shakespearean plays as *Twelfth Night, As You Like It,* and *The Merchant of Venice,* in Restoration comedies like *The Country Wife,* and in nineteenth-century farces such as *Dandy Dick* and *The Amazons*. On the other hand, female impersonation was rarely seen in regular drama. Only in Christmas pantomimes was the characterization of a rather oafish masculine female impersonation regularly included. Too accurate a portrayal of female mannerisms would have been construed as an affront to Victorian codes of sexual role playing.

The reviewers of the original production all indicated a certain amount of apprehension at the potential for an unsavory interpretation of the character. They also noted, however, that Penley's portrayal was delightfully proper. The critic for *The Athenaeum,* while calling Penley's performance of Babbs "artistic" and "droll," cautioned him not to "yield to temptation and accentuate a part which might easily be rendered repellant."[4] On the other hand, the critic for *The Saturday Review* expressed genuine surprise that Penley could be successful with such a role.

> In this country critical opinion and popular sentiment are equally opposed to the assumption of female characters by male actors. Not only has Mr. Penley played the part of an old lady, but he has made her the pivot of the play, and has drawn genuine laughter throughout three acts of a farcical comedy without a vestige of offence.[5]

The reviewer for *The Times* described the nature of Penley's successful characterization:

> In all such impersonations the besetting danger is vulgarity of treatment or suggestion. This Mr. Penley contrives to avoid. He does not seek to produce the strong-minded, red-nosed, masculine female who is accustomed to tread the boards in Christmas pantomime. He pretends merely to masquerade in the missing lady's character. The effect is not only inoffensive but in a high degree entertaining, especially for a holiday audience.[6]

In other words, Penley made Babbs acceptable by playing him as an irritated and more than reluctant accomplice who is not very good at female impersonation. After all, Babbs has never acted before. Thus, Penley's original portrayal (which has become the traditional interpretation) had Babbs gesturing, sitting, standing and walking like a man. When Babbs tries to raise the pitch of his voice upon first meeting Kitty and Amy, it cracks horribly; for the rest of the play he uses his normal male speaking voice. In addition, Penley's own farcical appearance was incorporated into the character—"Small, about five feet three to five feet six at most, *humorous* face"—yielding anything but an attractive aunt.

In addition to the unique aspects of character provided by the disguise, Babbs has been given other eccentricities that further describe him as an original victim. First and most intriguingly, there is something of the knave about him. While he endures the physical and psychological abuse of Jack and Charley, this victim has occasion to return some of the punishment. He takes

Figure 11. W.S. Penley as Babbs in the Original Production of *Charley's Aunt*, 1892
(Photograph from the Mander and Mitcheson Theatre Collection)

playful and sometimes vengeful delight in being conspicuously close to the young girls in Jack and Charley's presence, counterpunches with an occasional kick to their shins, and threatens them at all times with giving up the whole masquerade. Nor does he ever miss a chance to humiliate Spettigue in any way he can.

In order to maintain Babbs as a sympathetic character in the midst of his knavish activities, he is given another trait uncommon to British farce victims—tenderness. It surfaces briefly but sufficiently in Act III as Ela describes the young man (Babbs) that recently saved her and her dying father from destitution:

> ELA: But the noblest man I ever knew was shy, and oh, so kind! He got to know how papa had become so ill-and so poor-and lost a large sum of money to him at cards, Auntie thinks, on purpose. I often wondered why they played cards, and papa so ill too, but when I asked the doctor if it wasn't doing harm, he said, "Not the game that was being played." (III-99)

Finally, Babbs is given the highest social status of any character victimized in Victorian farce.[7] But as Lord Fancourt Babberly he has been rendered temporarily broke by his generosity to Ela's father. Thus, he has been farcically reduced to filching champagne from his chums and even borrowing the money for tipping Brassett, the butler.

Brassett is also a British farce original. Formerly, major comic and farcical servants were distinguished by their lack of sophistication. They dropped their "aitches," were loyal only in relation to their salaries (which varied directly with their low IQs and lack of breeding). Functionally, it was most often their scheming that affected the intrigue. Brassett, on the other hand, was the first in a long line of dignified, imperturbable British butlers that became the mainstay of the farces and comedies from Oscar Wilde to Noel Coward. Brassett is always calm and under control—even as the desperate predicament of his masters swirls around him. He is loyal to Jack and Charley and delightfully indulgent of their wild excesses.

The other characters are, for the most part, the undifferentiated stereotypes of the pre-Pinero farces. The young lovers are the standard mischievous adolescents who are nearly indistinguishable from their counterparts in hundreds of other farces. Only their better breeding and their proximity to Fancourt Babberly makes them slightly more noticeable. Spettigue is the typical old man of farce who has his romantic eye on his young ward. Sir Francis is another member of Victorian farces' veritable regiment of handsome army officers of the late Indian Service.

Only Donna Lucia seems to show the influence of Pinero's female characterizations. She is independently wealthy, self-assured, and she dominates all the others when she is onstage. After all, she is controlling the intrigue for her own amusement; she is the one to finally pull Charley, Jack, and Babbs out of their predicament and even promises that she will provide for the defeated Spettigue "the most profound reparation my influence can make" (III-107).

In the final analysis, though, the characters of *Charley's Aunt* are primarily straight men to the outrageously eccentric and unique clown that is Fancourt Babberly. These characters, however, are only as straight as their absurd inability to recognize Babbs through his inept impersonation. Not only are the girls gleefully taken in by the disguise, but Sir Francis and Spettigue actually propose marriage to the funny-looking matron who talks and moves like a man.

The extended sentiment inherent in Babbs and others that might also tend to reduce the farcical effect is, in the end, always undercut in traditional ways. For instance, it seems Jack can never get very far in creating a romantic mood with Kitty before she defuses the moment:

> JACK: No! Those stolen moments in the garden by ourselves were the very happiest of all my life, and out there in the moonlight—ah, moonlight is the true atmosphere for—for sentiment.
> KITTY: I wonder how many people have said that? (I-25)

In addition to its other uniquely structured aspects, *Charley's Aunt* has the distinction of being perhaps the only Victorian farce with memorable, even quotable dialogue. While some of this language borders on wit, it is basically pure, farcical nonsense diction of the funniest kind.

Undoubtedly, the most famous and oft-repeated phrase from *Charley's Aunt* is the recurring line, "I'm Charley's aunt, from Brazil where the nuts come from." Repeated five times in the course of the play, it becomes funnier in each new context, the final time being to the real Donna Lucia herself. Other famous one-line exclamations include Babbs' disclaimer, "I'm no ordinary woman," and his response to Donna Lucia's query as to whether he has any children: "Only a few—none to speak of." Brassett's memorable "College Boys'll do anything" more than any other line describes the overall probabilities of this farce.

While a standard assortment of such devices as consecutive asides, contradictory one-liners, puns, name jokes, and humorous vocalizations is used in *Charley's Aunt,* the most frequently employed type of effective dialogue might be called parrot speech. An elaboration of a standard music hall routine, parrot speech occurs when one character who is being secretly prompted by another repeats not only the intended promptings but the indignant asides as well. Used half a dozen times in the play, parrot speech occurs most often as Babbs is being prompted by Jack and Charley on what to say as Charley's bogus aunt:

> LORD FANCOURT: Of course, my dear. (*taking his arm from round her, quietly*) It was only
> my duty to see after the welfare of my poor brother's—
> JACK (*aside to Lord Fancourt, quickly*): Sister's you fool!
> LORD FANCOURT: (*to Amy, repeating*): Sister's, you fool—(*correcting himself*) Sister's (*with
> aggressive look at Jack*) and (*Amy*) brother-in-law's orphan girl.
> JACK (*aside, as before*): Boy! Boy!
> LORD FANCOURT (*to Amy*): Boy—Boy! (*aside to Jack*) I'll say twins in a minute. (I-37)

While such passages are perhaps not as quotable as some of the one-liners, they have remained memorable nonetheless. Moreover, much of the farcical spectacle in the play is quite as famous as the dialogue.

Visual humor figures largely in *Charley's Aunt;* Thomas used an assortment of the best *lazzi* associated with the British farce tradition and suited them all to the amazing pantomimic talents of W. S. Penley. In this regard, the most frequently used visual jokes in *Charley's Aunt* are of the knockabout variety. As he had proven in *The Private Secretary,* no one could endure more physical punishment more humorously than W. S. Penley. Therefore, Babbs, like Spalding, is punched (eight times), kicked (six times), pushed (seven times), tossed about, slapped, and even dropped to the floor as a chair is pulled out from under him. Having endured so much punishment, Babbs seems to hit back at the end of the play for all the victims of British farce:

> (*Donna Lucia hands her across to Lord Fancourt. Lord Fancourt takes Ela's left hand and
> tucks it in his arm and as they turn to go up center Lord Fancourt kicks the front of
> Charley's leg with his instep as he passes. Charley limps round behind ottoman to right of
> Amy.*) (III-108).

Ultimately, the farcical effect of all of this knockabout is heightened by the incongruity of it being visited upon a small person dressed up as an elderly woman.

The costume itself is the source of the most constant visual humor in the play. On opening night, Penley's appearance in a black satin dress, bonnet, fichu, and mittens veritably stopped the show; throughout the stalls could be seen plenty of real chaperones identically dressed. Murmurs were heard throughout the house: "How like Aunt Sarah!" "How like Aunt Jemima!"[8] Lurking underneath the matronly petticoats, of course, were a pair of trousers that constantly threatened to reveal themselves at highly inopportune moments.

Finally, the physical business that is most symbolic of *Charley's Aunt's* traditional British roots is that having to do with hats. There are no less than ten sight gags in the play involving hats that are knocked off, repeatedly struck, placed on Charley's foot, and used to hide all manner of incriminating objects like whiskey glasses and Babbs' male shoes. The hat routines culminate at the end of Act II when Babbs accords Spettigue's hat the most famous treatment ever given a chapeau in any play since Gilbert's *Wedding March:*

> *(Lord Fancourt deliberately pours tea into Spettigue's hat on chair of table, very neatly, without spilling any, all the time talking over his shoulder to Donna Lucia....*
> *Lord Fancourt pours cream into cup, then into hat, talking to Spettigue meanwhile.*
> *Suddenly discovering tea in hat, puts cup on table and lifts up hat.)*
> LORD FANCOURT: My hat, my hat! *(puts down milk jug, looks apologetically concerned, and takes hat)* I beg your pardon.
> *(He makes three circular movements with hat to mix the milk and tea, opens lid of teapot, pours hat to Spettigue. Spettigue takes hat. Lord Fancourt taps bottom of it. Brassett takes hat from Spettigue, who turns away wiping eye. Lord Fancourt gaily flips down lid of teapot and sits. Brassett exits to rooms with hat.) (II-82)*

That *Charley's Aunt* should extract so much laughter from hat *lazzi* seems only fitting for this, the most madcap farce of them all.

In its opening night review, *The Times* augured a "prosperous career" for *Charley's Aunt.*[9] But even the prophetic critic who made that prediction could not have foreseen its ultimate lasting success as the most revived farce in modern times. For despite its Victorian origins, *Charley's Aunt* has achieved a kind of artistic universality that transcends cultures and languages—surely the mark of a great work of art. In fact the Brandon Thomas family claimed that, as late as 1953, a day did not pass without a performance of *Charley's Aunt* somewhere in the world.[10] Perhaps the most remarkable production of *Charley's Aunt* took place in Cairo during the Second World War. Several actors of different nationalities accidentally met in Shepheard's Bar where they discovered that they had played in *Charley's Aunt* during their careers. They immediately agreed to give a production for charity, and since there was no one language that they all spoke, each performed in his own tongue. The audience of course had no trouble in following the proceedings, since they knew *Charley's Aunt* almost as well as the actors.

In its own time *Charley's Aunt* dominated the last decade of the nineteenth century—its four-year run finally coming to an end on December 19, 1896. But rather than serving as the inspiration for a new, vital direction for British farce as did *The Pink Dominos, The Private Secretary,* and *The Magistrate, Charley's Aunt* was the final culmination of the form's development. It was the last great Victorian farce much in the way that *A Pair of Spectacles* was the last great sentimental comedy. To use a structural metaphor—*Charley's Aunt* was the obligatory scene of the intriguing development of nineteenth-century British farce. All that remained to be played out was a rather quick resolution of its formerly overwhelming popularity.

The Decline of British Farce

In the last seven years of the nineteenth century, full-length British farce declined in popularity almost as quickly as it had appeared in 1875. Without the perspective of history, theatrical producers saw the success of *Charley's Aunt* as the dawn of yet another new age of farce popularity. They assumed that *Charley's Aunt* was *the* formula. In the hands of hack writers looking to turn a quick profit, farce became imitative rather than derivative.

At first the public accepted one or two of the better *Charley's Aunt* imitations, but the formula soon became overly familiar and, on the whole, theatre-goers began to lose interest—despite the initial rush to produce more farces. Max Beerbohm, whose brother was a major farce actor, spoke for the public and the critics alike when he wrote:

> I have no prejudice against farce as a dramatic form; on the contrary, I love it. I have even seen, in recent years, farces which moved me to much laughter. *Charley's Aunt* was one: it had an excellent idea, excellently developed. For a similar reason, I delighted in *The Magistrate,* as I delighted in all Mr. Pinero's farces. . . . the stock situations of farce, were used in such a way that they became new and distinguished. It is only when a farce is written without any new central idea, without wit, without humour, with nothing but a repetition of all the stock situations peppered over with as many new vulgarities as the author is original enough to invent, that I am unable to enjoy the two or three hours spent in witnessing it. Unfortunately, in the English theatre, almost all farces are of this kind.[11]

Thus, between 1892 and 1900 over 120 full-length farces were produced in London of which only nineteen played more than one-hundred performances. Of those nineteen farces, only four played more than two hundred performances.

Of these four moderately successful farces, Arthur Law's *The New Boy* and Robert Buchanan's and Charles Marlowe's *The Strange Adventures of Miss Brown,* are basically imitations of *Charley's Aunt. The New Boy,* which opened at Terry's Theatre on February 21, 1894, is a disguise farce that relied largely for its effect on the personal idiosyncrasies of its actor-manager, Weedon Grossmith (1852–1919). Grossmith played a little man who had the misfortune to marry a widow older and much larger than himself. Through coincidental circumstances the little man loses his fortune and the couple is plunged into poverty. Suddenly it is learned that the wife has been willed a large sum of money that she may receive only if she is single. Therefore she concocts a plan to pass her husband off as her son, whereupon she starts calling him "Freddy," dresses him in little sailor suits and Eton jackets, and sends him to school with the other little boys. The critic for *The Times* reported that Law's play "kept the house in roars of laughter," and predicted that *The New Boy* "is probably destined for a long run."[12]

The Strange Adventures of Miss Brown, which debuted at The Vaudeville on June 17, 1895, is an even more blatant copy of *Charley's Aunt.*

This farce concerns a dashing young cavalry officer named Captain Courtnay who has married Angela Brightwell, a ward in chancery, without having first obtained the necessary permission. In order to elude lawyers and policemen pursuing him, the Captain shaves off his mustache, dresses up as a schoolgirl, and sneaks into the girls' academy where his wife is being held captive. The results are predictable. The critic for *The Theatre,* for one, took the authors to task for their unabashed farcical copying: "For, truth to tell, neither in the matter of originality nor of wit have they been too prodigal.... At one moment we have a suggestion of *Don Juan,* at another *The Magistrate* is recalled, while at every turn the unmistakable influence of *Charley's Aunt* can be detected."[13]

The only other farces to achieve a modicum of success in the last years of the century were of foreign origin. Seymor Hicks's *A Night Out,* which opened at The Vaudeville on April 29, 1896, and ran for 529 performances, is an adaptation of George Feydeau's and Maurice Desvalliere's *Hôtel du libre échange.* It stands as the first introduction of Feydeau's work in London. The last successfully produced farce of the nineteenth century was written by the famous American dramatist, George Broadhurst. His disguise farce, *What Happened to Jones,* opened at The Strand on July 12, 1898, and had a moderately successful run of 328 performances.

The reality of the situation was that public enthusiasm for the full-length farce began to decline rapidly in the last five years of the century. As it became apparent that blatant imitations of *Charley's Aunt* would not draw, managers and writers fell back on older formulas in their attempts to attract the lucrative crowds that had patronized farce for the previous twenty years. Unfortunately, none of the old, proven farcical methods could find a successful place in the late nineties.

The easiest and seemingly safest route to take was the revival of the formerly popular farces; but all of the revivals attempted in the nineties failed miserably. *Dr. Bill,* an adaptation from the French of Albert Carré and Hamilton Aidé, had run for 210 performances at The Avenue Theatre in 1890. In late 1894, C. H. Hawtrey revived this farce at The Court Theatre. But what was entertaining in the pre-*Charley's Aunt* period seemed to have aged considerably in five years. In revival it lasted for only twenty-six performances.

The other revivals fared not much better. William Greet produced *The Private Secretary* at The Avenue Theatre on March 9, 1895, in its third and least successful revival, lasting only for fifty-six nights. Similarly, Weedon Grossmith's revival of *The New Boy* lasted for only one-tenth of its original run, and the last attempted farce revival of the century, Walter Tyrrell's production of Grundy's *The Arabian Nights* (Novelty, July 15, 1896) played for less than a week before closing.

Once-successful farceurs did not fare much better with their new works. Arthur Law's first effort after *The New Boy* was another vehicle for Weedon

Grossmith titled *The Ladies Idol.* It opened at The Vaudeville on April 18, 1895, and closed less than two months later. The critic for *The Theatre* exhibited a talent for understatement in referring to Law's current venture as "perhaps a little less fortunate" than *The New Boy.*[14] F. C. Burnand, the former master of adaptation, was described in that same journal as approaching his latest farcical effort, *Mrs. Ponderbury's Past* (Avenue, November 2, 1895), with "a faint heart." He was also accused of being "regretably sparing in the distribution of those witty lines which have gained for him a widespread reputation as a humorist."[15] Sidney Grundy's "original farce," *The Late Mr. Castello,* which lasted for two months at The Comedy Theatre beginning December 28, 1895, was dismissed as "half a century behind the times."[16] Similarly, Harry Paulton, who had achieved success with *Niobe, All Smiles,* failed miserably with his original farcical comedy, *In a Locket,* which debuted at The Strand on September 16, 1895, and closed fifty-four days later. Paulton's play is an old-fashioned confusion farce that relies on a heavy use of equivocation for forwarding the action. Audiences had tired of this type of farce more than ten years earlier.

Moreover, the popular writers of extreme farces who had been the adventurous experimenters with the form in the eighties could not seem to find a new method for theatrical success in the nineties. Mark Melford's *The Jerry Builder* (Strand, June 19, 1894) was actually reported in *The Times* as being "intolerably dull."[17] It lasted for only sixteen performances. J. H. Darnley fared no better. His extreme farce, *Mrs. Dexter* (Strand, February 28, 1894), ran for barely two weeks before it closed. Wrote *The Times:* "If bustle and hurryscurry could take the place of wit, character, or story, then Mr. J. H. Darnley's new farce, *Mrs. Dexter,* would be an excellent piece of its kind. It is all flurry and excitement with a very small substratum of incident."[18] Darnley's *Shadows on the Blind* (Terry's, April 30, 1898), an object-chase farce, was even less successful, playing for a total of nine performances. In 1897, *The Times* literally wrote the obituary for such extreme plays in its review of Glen MacDonough's "extravagant farce," *The Prodigal Father* (Strand, February 1, 1897): "perhaps the taste of the public favours fun of a less extravagant character than it did ten years ago or than is here provided."[19]

Not even famous actors, who had saved many a weak farce in the past with their humorous playing, could work their old magic on the new farces of the nineties. The likes of C. H. Hawtrey, Lottie Venne, and Nina Boucicault could not save R. C. Carton's original farce, *A White Elephant* (Comedy, November 19, 1896). Lasting barely three months, the play afforded these experienced performers very few opportunities. Lottie Venne did not even appear until a few minutes before the final curtain. Willie Edouin must have thought that he had a surefire idea for a hit when he had Fenton MacKay build a farce around his most famous characterization: Heathen Chinee from the twenty-year-old burlesque, *Blue Beard.* The result was *Qwong Hi,* which opened at Terry's on June 27, 1895. If anything it turned out to be an unqualified disaster, lasting less than four weeks. Similarly, Fred Horner's farcical comedy, *The Sunbury Scandal* (Terry's, June 11, 1896), was so bad that during its five-day run Beerbohm Tree played the part of Carl Rottenstein under the name of "Mr. Robb Harwood." Fanny Brough, whose "unflagging endeavor" might have saved the piece, was according to one critic "handicapped by the incomprehensibility of the part."[20]

In view of the consistent failure of farces produced in London in the last seven years of the decade, entreprenurial enthusiasm for the form began to wane. From a post-*Charley's Aunt* high of twenty-five farces produced in 1895, the number fell to sixteen in 1896, fourteen in 1897, twelve in 1898, and finally eleven in 1899. These figures do show, however, that a significant number of managers were still speculating on the chance that they might find another hit like *Charley's Aunt* or even a more modest one like *The New Boy* or *A Night Out*. The more successful speculators, however, were investing in new forms of drama that began to catch the public fancy in these years— dramatic forms that were largely anathema to the nature of farce.

First, new varieties of comedy had evolved from Pinero's so-called character farces like *Dandy Dick* and *The Cabinet Minister*. The most successful variety was a genuine comedy of manners that drew its inspiration from the lighter, more distinctly British aspects of Pinero's writing. These comedies made use of the farcical well-made form, but described a universe free from the capricious machinations of farce—one in which the object of ridicule was the mannered behavior by which Englishmen had freely chosen to live. There is no desperate insanity at which to laugh in these plays, but rather the traditional human weaknesses that have always been the preserve of non-sentimental comedy, such as greed, selfishness, prejudice, narrow-mindedness, egocentricity, and empty social creeds. In this sense, then, Oscar Wilde's *The Importance of Being Earnest* is a comedy, though it is often referred to as a farce. Wilde's "Trivial Comedy for Serious People in Three Acts" opened on Valentine's Day, 1895, at The St. James Theatre. Even though the world of *Earnest* is inverted in the Gilbertian manner of "topseyturveydom," it is not a world that is incomprehensible to the characters; it is all perfectly sensible to them, and no one has trouble with his or her sanity. The emphasis, as in most comedies, is on what they are doing (i.e., manners) rather than on what is happening to them (i.e., victimization). In its original run, *Earnest* did not do much better than the farces against which it was competing, lasting for only ninety-one performances. More successful with the new comedies of manners were Henry Arthur Jones and Arthur Wing Pinero, both of whom ridiculed a less topsey-turvey society than Wilde. Jones achieved moderate success with *The Case of the Rebellious Susan* (Criterion, November 3, 1884) which ran for 164 performances, and with his final comedy of the century, *The Manoeuvres of Jane* (Haymarket, October 29, 1898) which lasted for nine months. Pinero's most popular comedy also occurred in the last years of the decade. His *The Gay Lord Quex* (Globe, April 8, 1899) stands as the most successful laughing comedy of the century with its run of 304 performances.

The other variety of laughing comedy to appear in the last years of the century were the thesis comedies of George Bernard Shaw. Unlike the comedies of manners, Shaw's plays did not make much of an impact on the public consciousness in the 1890s. His only publicly produced play, *Arms and the Man,* opened at The Avenue Theatre on April 21, 1894, as a "Romantic Comedy" and lasted for only seventy-five performances—a perhaps significant run that was completely obscured that year by the successes of *Charley's Aunt* and *The New Boy.*

Still, Shaw was an instrumental force in the decline of British farce through his vociferous, passionate, published criticism of the form. His objections, which struck at the very purpose of farce, appeared in the May 9, 1896, edition of *The Saturday Review*—a journal which had published so many favorable reviews of farces:

> To laugh without sympathy is a ruinous abuse of a noble function; and the degradation of any race may be measured by the degree of their addiction to it . . . we find people who would not join in the laughter of a crowd of peasants at the village idiot, or tolerate the public flogging or pillorying of a criminal, booking seats to shout with laughter at a farcical comedy, which is, at bottom, the same thing—namely, the deliberate indulgence of that horrible, derisive joy in humiliation and suffering which is the beastliest element in human nature.[21]

After twenty years of British criticism that dealt with farce on a basis equal to other genres, the old methods of derogating the "harmless laughter" of farce had begun anew.

Another particularly audible voice that echoed Shaw's objections was that of J. T. Grein, founder in 1891 of The Independent Theatre Club, an organization devoted to the non-profit production of the "drama of ideas" which included Shavian comedy, naturalistic foreign plays, and native "problem plays." About farce he wrote:

> The actors work without will and like Trojans; they rush about the stage as if panic had stricken them; they blurt out their wild bits of dialogue as if under pneumatic pressure; they shout, gesticulate, play tricks, gamble with the irresponsible abandon of an amiable lunatic asylum let loose; they give us no time to think, to analyze or to criticize.[22]

Grein's analysis of the basic theatricality of farce, while accurate, was meant as unfavorable criticism. Theatricality was exactly anathema to the intentions of the realistic drama which sought to hide all vestiges of artificiality in an attempt to portray the very serious truth.

That there was an audience for such plays became apparent with the successful production of Pinero's trend-setting problem play, *The Second*

Mrs. Tanqueray, which opened at the St. James Theatre on May 27, 1893, and remained popular for nearly a year. In 1897, the production of Henry Arthur Jones's *The Liars,* which debuted on June 10, had an equally lucrative run of 322 performances. In the same year P. M. Augustin Filon, the twenty-five-year observer of British drama, speculated on the relative success of the Norwegian-style drama in London:

> However that may be, the time is approaching when the Norwegian drama will pay. Not, of course, like *Charley's Aunt!* One must not expect too much when one has only genius. Ibsen can and should keep alive without robbing or coveting a single one of Mr. Penley's spectators.[23]

The fact is, however, that Filon was writing his opinion just as *Charley's Aunt* was about to close and reveal what its overwhelming success had obscured— full-length stage farce was losing its appeal.

This is not to say, however, that farce in general was losing favor—only the three-act Victorian farce as it had evolved over the previous twenty-five years. The human race has always found a means for laughing at the ridiculousness of its victimization by capricious circumstance. And in the last years of the nineteenth century a medium more accommodating to farce made its portentous appearance—motion pictures. What the nineteenth-century farce writer could present only as offstage spectacle could graphically be put on film by the cinematic farceur.

The possibilities of this potentially revolutionary outlet for the farcical imagination were illustrated by a half-minute film made by the Lumière brothers in 1895. It shows a man watering a lawn. A child steps on the hose, stopping the water. The man looks into the nozzle just as the child takes his foot off of the hose and the man gets squirted in the face. In his article "A Slapstick Renaissance," Walker Stuart describes the particular farcical advantages of motion pictures:

> In the new medium, it was possible to capture a considerable breadth of comic action in any locale, to focus attention on the smallest significant detail, and to combine the resultant pieces of film in whatever lengths and whatever sequence might be necessary to create the maximum comic effect. The result was a comedy form that has extracted more laughter from more people than any other amusement ever devised with the possible exception of tickling.[24]

In light of these qualities, it is not surprising that *Charley's Aunt* has been filmed four times, making it one of the most remade movies ever.[25]

By the turn of the century managers and especially playwrights recognized a kind of stigma attached to the term "farce." Also, since laughter had returned to comedy, the distinction between the two forms was no longer as apparent as it had been in the sentimental age. Thus, after 1900, many farces were labeled as comedies.

In light of all the bad press that farce was getting, G. K. Chesterton felt obligated in 1900 to write that rarity of dramatic criticism, a defense of farce. "Some day, perhaps," he wrote, "when the present narrow phase of aesthetics has ceased to monopolize the name, the glory of the farcical art may become fashionable."[26]

The Dramatic Phenomenon of Late Victorian Farce

The appearance of full-length British farce in 1875 was a product of rapidly changing times. The industrial revolution brought on a population explosion that changed and diversified theatrical marketing practices. Victorianism provided a rigid code of domestic morals for the daily lives of the new masses—morals that were upheld by the serious drama of the time (i.e., melodrama and sentimental comedy) and lampooned by the humorous (i.e., farce and burlesque). The habits of Queen Victoria also brought the fashionable audiences back to the theatre in the eighteen sixties and seventies, where they were treated to the three-act farce as the main attraction rather than in its traditional role of afterpiece.

The new full-length version retained many elements traditional to British farce, such as (1) a single-minded purpose of arousing laughter; (2) a capriciously malevolent universe that victimizes an undeserving protagonist to the point of insanity; (3) domestic subject matter; (4) a plot unified by action; (5) undifferentiated characterizations; (6) humorous nonsense language; and (7) a substantial reliance for effect on spectacle. New structural elements were added in stages as the three-act farce evolved.

Between 1875 and 1884 the so-called farcical comedy dominated. These farces were mostly deodorized adaptations of the French originals of Scribe, Sardou, Labiche, and others. Inspired by the 1877 adaptation *The Pink Dominos,* these English farcical comedies are distinguished by well-made play structures, victimizations incited by misunderstanding attendant upon precise manipulation of dramatic irony, low-level, noneccentric characterizations of upper-middle-class types, sound-effectual dialogue, and the highest proportions of laughter-producing spectacle yet seen in British farce.

The ten-year apprenticeship that the British farceurs spent in adapting French farces served them well: the years 1885-1894 were dominated by the writing and production of distinctively native farces that were inspired largely by the Court farces of Arthur Wing Pinero and the Globe farces produced by C. H. Hawtrey. In these original British farces the plots of misunderstanding gave way to those incited by less equivocal intentional deceptions which required more eccentric characterizations of upper-class types (i.e., knavish adolescents; unfrugal, independent wives; and respected professionals). These farces were also often distinguished by elegant farce language that was rendered as a kind of brilliant, nonsensical antiwit.

The increased emphasis on character, motives, and language brought this type of farce close to the specific realm of comedy. In fact, it may be concluded that the vitality and popularity of the three-act Victorian farce were particularly instrumental in bringing about the re-emergence of laughing comedy in the 1890s—after a 175-year domination of the sentimental variety. It is ironic, then, that the traditional view of this period holds that since the comedies of Shaw, Wilde, Pinero, and Jones appeared in the late 1890s, the preceding years must have lacked significant dramatic initiative.

In actuality, as this study has shown, the eighteen seventies, eighties, and early nineties were dramatically alive with farce production in every aspect, from master-writers to fortune-making entrepreneurs and virtuoso actors. Indeed, entire theatrical careers were devoted to making and producing native farce. Furthermore, the twenty-five-year domination of full-length British farce is not unlike that of other genres in productive periods of British drama, such as that of Shakespeare and his contemporaries, and the comic plays written during the era of the Restoration. Like these exceptional periods, the Golden Age of British farce produced its masterpieces which are also worthy of revival: *The Snowball, Confusion, The Private Secretary, The Magistrate, The Schoolmistress. Dandy Dick, The Barrister, The Solicitor, The New Boy,* and, of course, *Charley's Aunt.*

In its own time the phenomenal development of the full-length British farce came to a symbolic end in 1900 when W. S. Penley opened the former Novelty Theatre as The Great Queen Theatre, appeared in revivals of his most successful roles, and retired from the stage at the end of the year.

Productions of late Victorian farce have become intermittently fashionable since its heyday. Pinero's *The Magistrate* was revived in London at The Cambridge Theatre in September 1969 by the Chichester Festival in a production starring Sir Alistair Sim. The Court farces have remained in the English speaking repertories since. More than any other factor, the success of these productions has been responsible for the recent scholarly and entrepreneurial interest in nineteenth-century British farce. And, unlike virtually every other British play of the nineteenth century, *Charley's Aunt* has never left the world repertory.

Certainly there is something universal about these British farces of the late nineteenth century. J. H. Darnley, Britain's master of the extreme farce, understood the nature of the farcical predicament as well as anyone when he wrote of his protagonist in *The Solicitor:* "He is simply the victim of circumstances, my dear; we all are, more or less" (II-38). Like Darnley, the British theatre people and theatre-goers of the late Victorian period were particularly entertained by this idea. In truth, the picture of a man as an undeserving victim, driven to the limits of his sanity by a predicament too nonsensical to explain rationally, is a spectacle that transcends period, language, race, social condition, and all national boundaries.

Figure 12.   1910 London Poster for *Charley's Aunt*, Still in Use Today
(*Photograph from the Mander and Mitcheson Theatre Collection*)

Notes

Introduction

1. Allardyce Nicoll's "Handlist" of plays in his survey, *A History of the British Drama 1660–1900* (Cambridge: Cambridge University Press, 1959), lists over 3000 plays labeled as some kind of farce between 1800 and 1900.

2. Allardyce Nicoll, *A History of English Drama 1660–1900*, V (Cambridge: Cambridge University Press, 1959), p. 105.

3. Nicoll, p. 105.

4. William Archer, *Play-Making* (Boston: Boston, Small, Maynard and Company, 1912), p. 284.

5. P. M. Augustin Filon, *The English Stage* (1898, rpt. London: Benjamin Blom, 1969), p. 72.

6. Eric Bentley, *The Life of the Drama* (New York: Atheneum, 1964), p. 254.

7. Lynton Hudson, *The English Stage 1850–1950* (London: Harrap, 1951), p. 102.

8. Clayton Hamilton, "Farces and Melodramas," *The Forum*, 41 (1909), p. 25.

9. Joseph Wood Krutch, "The Fundamentals of Farce," *Theatre Arts*, July 1952, p. 92.

10. Eric Bentley, "The Psychology of Farce," *Let's Get a Divorce and Other Plays* (New York: Hill and Wang, 1958), p. viii.

11. Werner Klemm, *Die Englische Farce im 19 Jahrhundert* (Berne: A. Francke, 1946) and Leo Hughes, *A Century of English Farce* (Princeton: Princeton University Press, 1956). Recently, two general works on the subject of dramatic farce have been published: Albert Bermel's *Farce: A History from Aristophanes to Woody Allen* (New York: Simon and Schuster, 1982) and Jessica Milner Davis's *Farce* (London: Methuen, 1978). Bermel devotes only four pages to discussing nineteenth-century British farce. Davis's concise analytical work is Number 39 in Methuen's *The Critical Idiom* Series. She classifies farces into categories: humiliation-farce, quarrel-farce, circular-farce, talisman-farce, and snowball-farce.

12. Michael Booth, "Introduction," *English Plays of the Nineteenth Century: Farces* (Oxford: Clarendon Press, 1973), IV, 18.

Chapter 1

1. Quoted in Leo Hughes, "The Early Career of Farce in the Theatrical Vocabulary," University of Texas Studies in English, No. 20 (1940), p. 95.

2. In *The Winterbottoms! or My Aunt, the Dowager* (1837), William Moncrief anticipates *Charley's Aunt* by fifty-five years when Frank Jekyll makes his servant, Jeffrey, dress up as his aunt, the Dowager Lady Winterbottom, in order to win the hand of his true love.

3. See Michael R. Booth, ed., "Introduction," *English Plays of the Nineteenth Century: Farces* (Oxford: The Clarendon Press, 1973), IV, clxvi-clxvii.

4. Augustin Filon, *The English Stage* (New York: Benjamin Blom, 1969), p. 207.

5. Aunts and uncles were the most common sources of trouble. Countless farces with such titles as *Aunt Charlotte's Maid* (1858) by J. M. Morton, *My Aunt's Husband* (1858) by Charles Selby, and *A Model Uncle* (1858) by S. Z. M. Strauss were performed in this period.

6. The moral and sentimental intent of the comedies, however, dictated that the initial complication be the direct ethical responsibility of the protagonist. In a sense, comedy was prescriptive and didactic, while farce was merely descriptive.

7. In an anonymous *Times* review of James Albery's *Chiseling* (1870) the critic noted the passing of the afterpiece: "But the glories of the one-act farce are now passed away. In the days of its pomp and pride its place in the programme was after the substantial drama with which the evening commenced, and it was commonly followed by another piece of comparative solidity. Now it opens the evening's entertainment and heads the programme of nearly every theatre appropriated to comedy, but it is generally understood that nobody will go to see it." Quoted in *The Dramatic Works of James Albery,* ed. Wyndham Albery (London, 1935), p. 585.

8. P.M. Augustin Filon, *The English Stage* (1898 rpt. London: Benjamin Blom, 1969), p. 96.

9. H. J. Byron, *Not Such a Fool as He Looks,* in *French's Acting Editions* (London, 1868), CXX, 1.

10. Byron, p. 47.

11. Byron's other successful comedies of this sort include *Partners for Life* (1871), *Old Soldiers* (1873), *Sour Grapes* (1873), *An American Lady* (1874), *Old Sailors,* and *Our Boys* (1875).

12. Byron strongly urged the production of Robertson's *Society* at the Prince of Wales' Theatre, after it had been refused by Buckstone at the Haymarket as worthless. Anonymous, "Portraits, VI—Mr. Henry J. Byron," *The Theatre,* 1 October 1878, p. 213.

13. His other farces include *The Haunted Man* (1849), *The Clockmaker's Hat* (1855), *Peace at Any Price* (1856), *The Cantab* (1861), *Not at All Jealous* (1871), and *A Row in the House* (1883). See Nicoll, pp. 546–47.

14. Tom W. Robertson, *A Breach of Promise,* in *French's Acting Editions* (London, 1869), CXXVIII, 1.

15. Robertson, p. 5.

16. Allardyce Nicoll, *The British Drama* (London: Harrap, 1958), p. 124.

17. "French Authors and English Adapters," *The Theatre,* December 1878, p. 329.

18. W. Davenport Adams, rev. of *The Gay City* by George Sims, *The Theatre,* October 1881, p. 237.

19. John Russell Taylor, *The Rise and Fall of the Well-Made Play* (New York: Hill and Wang, 1967), p. 32.

20. In a volume of his dramatic works published in 1841, Bulwer-Lytton described the nature of British sentimental comedy. "In our age," he wrote, "men are more earnest than in that of the old artificial comedy.... in 1840 we know that all life at least is not a jest. In the old comedy there is a laugh at everything most serious.... It is precisely because the present age is more thoughtful, that Comedy, in its reflection of the age must be more faithful to the chequered diversities of existence and go direct to its end through humours to truth, no matter whether its path lie through smiles or tears." Quoted in Nicoll, *British Drama,* p. 120.

21. H. J. Byron, *Our Boys,* in *French's Acting Editions* (London, 1884), CXVI, p. 21.

22. Anonymous rev. of *Our Boys* by H. J. Byron, *The Illustrated Sporting and Dramatic News.* 23 January 1875, p. 395.

23. Anonymous rev. of *Our Boys* by H. J. Byron, *The Theatre,* October 1878, p. 213.

24. See "Our Playbox," rev. of *Comrades* by Brandon Thomas, *The Theatre,* February 1883, 108–11.

25. W. S. Gilbert, *Tom Cobb, or Fortune's Toy,* in *French's Acting Editions* (London, 1975), CXVI, 1.

26. Gilbert, *Tom Cobb,* p. 3. All subsequent quotations from this play will be noted only by the act and page number in parentheses immediately following the quotation.

27. The written promise of marriage, which was considered a legally binding contract in this period, was used as a common device for forwarding the action of the early farcical comedies.

28. William Archer, "Are We Advancing," *About the Theatre,* (London: T. F. Unwin, 1886), p. 276.

29. Anonymous rev. of *Tom Cobb, or Fortune's Toy* by W. S. Gilbert, *The Theatre,* May 1875, p. 597.

30. Filon, p. 145. Indeed, so cruel a farce would never be seen until the turbulent 1960s produced such existentialist farceurs as Joe Orton, David Halliwell, and Alan Ayckbourn.

31. Filon, p. 144.

32. W.S. Gilbert, *Engaged,* in *French's Acting Editions,* CXVII, p. 9. All subsequent quotations from this play will be noted only by the act and page number in parentheses immediately following the quotation.

33. On the other hand, the comedies of the period employed an opposite device, the sentimental undercut, to deflate the increasingly humorous episodes of these sentimental plays: e.g., Joseph Derrick's *Twins* (1884) and Sidney Grundy's *A Pair of Spectacles* (1890).

34. Clement Scott, rev. of *Engaged* by W. S. Gilbert, *The Theatre,* October 1877, p. 64.

35. Filon, p. 146.

36. Eric Bentley, *The Life of the Drama* (New York: Atheneum, 1964), p. 225.

Chapter 2

1. In Volume I of Nicoll's *Early Nineteenth Century Drama,* Percy Fitzgerald is quoted as observing that "the English Stage is virtually subsisting on the French as late as 1881." Nicoll, p. 78.

2. H.W. Fowler, *A Dictionary of Modern English Usage* (Oxford: Oxford University Press, 1965), p. 305.

3. William Archer, *English Dramatists of Today* (London: S. Low, Marston, Searle, and Rivington, 1882), pp. 85–86.

4. A *domino* is a long, loose, hooded cloak usually worn with a half-mask as a masquerade costume.

5. James Albery, *The Pink Dominos, The Dramatic Works of James Albery,* ed. Wyndham Albery (London, 1935), II, p. 274.

6. Quoted in *The Collected Works of James Albery,* II, 205–6.

7. Anonymous rev. of *The Pink Dominos* by James Albery, *The Theatre,* 4 April 1877, p. 45.

8. Ernest A. Bendall, rev. of *Themis, The Theatre,* May 1880, pp. 301–2.

9. Clement Scott, "French Authors and English Adaptors," *The Theatre,* December 1878, p. 331.

10. Filon, p. 86.

11. Clement Scott, rev. of *Divorce* by Robert Reece, *The Theatre,* March 1878, p. 173.

12. Clement Scott, rev. of *Betsy* by F.C. Burnand, *The Theatre,* September 1879, p. 107.

13. Comediettas were generally one-act rhetorical, humorous pieces (not unlike some Tudor interludes) in which the action usually concerns a young rake who finally convinces a reluctant young woman to marry him.

14. Sidney Grundy, "Dramatic Construction," *The Theatre,* April 1881, p. 208.

15. Grundy, p. 210.

16. Sidney Grundy, *The Snowball,* in *French's Acting Editions* (London, 1879), CXXXI, p. 45. All subsequent quotations from this play will be noted only by the act and page number in parentheses immediately following the quotation.

17. Nahum Tate used the occasion of the publication of his farce *A Duke and No Duke* (1685) to include a defense of farce. The essence of Tate's argument was that there are no strictures or patterns to be followed in the making of a farce. There is some irony in the fact that Tate, who defended farce on the basis of its formlessness, was succeeded by defenders who praised the virtues of well-made structuring.

18. E. A. Bendall, rev. of *Themis, The Theatre,* May 1880, p. 302.

19. E. A. Bendall, rev. of *The Member for Slocum* and *The Mother-in-law* by George Sims, *The Theatre,* May 1881, p. 364.

20. Clement Scott, rev. of *The Guv'nor* by E. G. Lankester, *The Theatre,* August 1880, pp. 114–16.

21. Grundy, "Dramatic Construction," p. 209.

22. Bergson pointed out that the snowball device is an inherently funny aspect of repetition: it is an "effect which grows by arithmetical progression, so that the cause, insignificant at the outset, culminates by a necessary evolution in a result as important as it is unexpected." Henri Bergson, "Laughter," *Comedy,* ed. Wylie Sypher (Garden City: Doubleday, 1956), p. 113.

23. Grundy, "Dramatic Construction," p. 209.

24. E.G. Lankester, *The Guv'nor,* in *French's Acting Editions* (London, 1880), p. 28.

25. F. C. Burnand, *Betsy,* in *French's Acting Editions* (London, 1879), CXXVIII, p. 53.

26. Quoted by Neil Simon, *Dick Cavett Show,* PBS, 14 December 1977.

27. Charles Hawtrey, *The Truth at Last* (London: T. Butterworth Ltd., 1924), p. 309.

28. H. J. Byron, *Uncle,* in *French's Acting Editions* (London, 1879), CXVII, p. 28.

29. Victoria was named Empress of India in 1876. Africa, America, and "out at sea" also served as refuges for unknown relatives.

30. In his play *The Sunshine Boys,* Neil Simon has the old vaudevillian, Ben Silverman, advise his nephew that "words with a 'K' in it are funny. ... If it doesn't have a 'K,' it's not funny. I'll tell you which words always get a laugh. ... Chicken is funny. Pickle is funny. Cupcake is funny... Tomato is *not* funny." *The Collected Plays of Neil Simon* (New York: Random House, 1979), pp. 333–34.

31. Quoted in *Camille and Other Plays,* ed. Stephen Stanton (New York: Hill and Wang, 1957), p. xxiii.

32. John Dennis Hurrell, "A Note on Farce," *Quarterly Journal of Speech,* XLV (December, 1959), pp. 426–30.

33. Walter Kerr, *Tragedy and Comedy* (Simon and Schuster: New York, 1967), p. 193.

34. The first British newspaper was Nathaniel Butler's *Weekly News* which was published from 1622–1641. The newspapers of the eighteenth century were mainly journals of high literary merit. *The Times* of London, with its more general coverage, began publication in 1785 and served a rather uneducated readership.

35. W. S. Gilbert, *On Bail* in *French's Acting Editions* (London, 1877), p. 37.

36. Rev. of *The Gay City* by George Sims, *The Theatre,* October 1881, p. 237.

37. Anonymous rev. of *The Glass of Fashion* by Sidney Grundy, *The Saturday Review,* 1 October 1883, p. 202.

38. Anonymous rev. of *Confusion* by Joseph Derrick, *The Saturday Review,* July 1883, p. 18.

39. Clement Scott, rev. of *Confusion* by Joseph Derrick, *The Theatre,* August 1883, p. 109.

40. Henry Morley, quoted by Allardyce Nicoll, *The History of Late Nineteenth Century English Drama* (Cambridge: Cambridge University Press, 1946), I, 159–60.

41. Joseph Derrick, *Confusion,* in *French's Acting Editions* (London, 1883), CXXXII, p. 34.

42. W. H. Pollock, "A Glance at the Stage," *National Review,* July 1885, p. 646.

Chapter 3

1. Charles H. Hawtrey, *The Truth at Last* (London: T. Butterworth, 1924), p. 27.

2. Clement Scott, rev. of *The Private Secretary* by C. H. Hawtrey, *The Theatre*, May 1885, p. 279.

3. Hawtrey, *The Truth at Last*, p. 111.

4. Charles Hawtrey, *The Private Secretary* (London, 1894), p. 3. Subsequent quotations from this play will be noted only by the act and page number in parentheses immediately following the quotation.

5. By 1888 Charles Fawcett saw fit to label his German adaptation, *Katti; The Family Help*, as a "Domestic Farce in Three Acts" to indicate the middle-class backgrounds of its characters.

6. Clement Scott, rev. of *The Private Secretary, The Theatre*, p. 451.

7. Hawtrey, *The Truth at Last*, p. 111.

8. H. Saville Clark, rev. of *The Pickpocket* by George Hawtrey, *The Theatre*, June 1886, p. 325.

9. P. M. Augustin Filon, *The English Stage* (1898, rpt. London: Benjamin, 1969), p. 208.

10. Throughout his career Pinero wrote fifty-seven dramatic works ranging from curtain-raisers to sentimental comedies, farces, romances, problem plays, and fantasies. In 1909 he became the first playwright to be knighted.

11. Anonymous rev. of *Impudence* by Arthur Wing Pinero, *The Saturday Review*, 6 August 1881, p. 171.

12. Anonymous rev. of *Impudence* by Arthur Wing Pinero, *The Graphic*, 6 August 1881, p. 150.

13. Anonymous rev. of *Girls and Boys* by Arthur Wing Pinero, *The Times*, 1 November 1882, p. 8.

14. Arthur Wing Pinero, "The Theatre of the Seventies," *The Eighteen-Seventies*, ed. Harley Granville-Barker (New York, 1929), p. 146.

15. Anonymous rev. of *Low Water* by Arthur Wing Pinero, *The Saturday Review*, 29 November 1884, p. 619.

16. Quoted in Taylor, p. 54.

17. Arthur Wing Pinero, *The Magistrate* (Boston: Walter H. Baker, 1892), p. 27. Subsequent quotations from this play will be noted only by the act and page number in parentheses immediately following the quotation.

18. The telephone was patented by Alexander Graham Bell in 1876–1877.

19. Anonymous rev. of *The Magistrate* by Arthur Wing Pinero, *The Theatre*, April 1885, p. 200.

20. Anonymous rev. of *The Magistrate* by Arthur Wing Pinero, *The Times*, 23 March 1885, pp. 414–15.

21. Anonymous rev. of *The Magistrate* by Arthur Wing Pinero, *The Saturday Review*, 28 March, 1885, p. 418.

22. Anonymous rev. of *The Magistrate* by Arthur Wing Pinero, *The Athenaeum*, 28 March 1885, p. 317.

23. Clement Scott, rev. of *The Magistrate* by Arthur Wing Pinero, *Illustrated London News*, 28 March 1885, p. 317.

24. Anonymous rev. of *The Magistrate* by Arthur Wing Pinero, *The New York Times*, 26 September 1885, p. 5.

25. Anonymous rev. of *The Schoolmistress* by Arthur Wing Pinero, *The Saturday Review*, 3 April 1886, pp. 472–73.

26. Arthur Wing Pinero, *The Schoolmistress* (Boston: Walter H. Baker, 1982), p. 45. Subsequent quotations from this play will be noted only by the act and page number in parentheses immediately following the quotation.

27. Anonymous rev. of *The Schoolmistress* by Arthur Wing Pinero, *The Times*, March 29, 1886, p. 7.

28. Clement Scott, rev. of *The Schoolmistress*, by Arthur Wing Pinero, *The Theatre*, January 1886, p. 269.

29. Arthur Wing Pinero, *Dandy Dick* (Boston: Walter H. Baker, 1893), p. 1. Subsequent quotations from this play will be noted only by the act and page number in parentheses immediately following the quotation.

30. Anonymous rev. of *Dandy Dick* by Arthur Wing Pinero, *The Athenaeum*, 5 February 1887, p. 201.

31. Pinero wrote one last piece for the Court Theatre called *The Amazons*, which opened 7 March 1893. Labeled "a farcical romance," the play is more of an eccentric love story and exhibits none of the definitive, traditional farcical aspects. Produced by Arthur Chudleigh with a new company of actors, the play ran for only 111 performances before it closed.

32. Arthur Wing Pinero, *The Cabinet Minister* (Boston: Walter H. Baker, 1893), pp. 312–13. Subsequent quotations from this play will be noted only by the act and page number in parentheses immediately following the quotation.

33. Anonymous rev. of *The Cabinet Minister* by Arthur Wing Pinero, *The Saturday Review*, 26 April 1890, p. 501.

34. Clement Scott, rev. of *The Pair of Spectacles* by Sidney Grundy, *The Theatre*, April 1890, p. 102.

35. Quoted in *A Digest of 500 Plays*, ed. Theodore Shank (New York: Crowell-Collier Press, 1963), p. 102.

36. Anonymous rev. of *The Pink Dominos* by James Albery, *The Times*, 25 Nov. 1889. Quoted in *The Dramatic Works of James Albery*, ed. Wyndham Albery (London, 1935), pp. 205–6.

37. Edward A. Morton, "Comedy at the Court," *The Theatre*, September 1887, pp. 142–43.

38. "Nita's First," wrote the critic for *The Theatre*, "is surely far more amusing and more truly ludicrous than many that have gone before." April 1884, p. 218.

39. Charles Thomas, *The Paper Chase* (London: Samuel French, 1888), Thomas, p. 15.

40. Thomas, p. 9.

41. Percy Fitzgerald, rev. of *The Deputy Registrar* by Ralph Lumley and Horace Sedger, *The Theatre*, Jan. 1889, p. 63.

42. Mark Melford, *Turned Up* (London: Samuel French, 1891), p. 44. In this period the racial butt of jokes shifted away from the Irish to the Blacks and Jews.

43. The undoubtedly shocking spectacle of a black woman married to a white man was softened for the Victorian audiences of the eighties and nineties by the nature of Cleopatra's color: "Papa," asks Medway's daughter, "Is she very black?" "No, my dear," he replies, "not so (damned) black as—as my hat—sort of octoroon. Fact, she's quite fair as niggers go" (II-31).

44. Anonymous rev. of *Turned Up* by Mark Melford, *The Times,* 18 February 1891, p. 4.

45. Melford, p. 42.

46. Anonymous rev. of *Stop Thief* by Mark Melford, *The Theatre,* Dec. 1889, p. 305.

47. J. H. Darnley, *The Barrister* (London: Samuel French, 1887), p. 27.

48. Cecil Howard, rev. of *The Barrister* by J. H. Darnley, *The Theatre,* October 1887, p. 214.

49. J. H. Darnley, *The Balloon* (London: Samuel French, 1889), pp. 48–49.

50. Anonymous rev. of *Wanted, A Wife* by J. H. Darnley, *The Theatre,* July 1890, p. 34.

51. Anonymous rev. of *The Solicitor* by J. H. Darnley, *The Theatre,* August 1890, p. 86.

Chapter 4

1. Amy Brandon-Thomas, Silvia Brandon-Thomas, and Jevan Brandon-Thomas, "Program Notes," *Souvenir Program of Charley's Aunt,* Sixtieth Anniversary Production, Coronation Year 1953, p. 1.

2. Brandon Thomas, *Charley's Aunt,* ed. E. P. Wood, (London: Heineman Educational Books, 1969) p. 108. All subsequent quotations from this play will be noted only by the act and page number in parentheses immediately following the quotation.

3. Anonymous rev. of *Charley's Aunt* by Brandon Thomas, *The Saturday Review,* 24 December 1892, p. 741.

4. Anonymous rev. of *Charley's Aunt* by Brandon Thomas, *The Athenaeum,* 31 December 1892, p. 931.

5. *The Saturday Review,* p. 741.

6. Anonymous rev. of *Charley's Aunt* by Brandon Thomas, *The Times,* 22 Dec. 1892, p. 10.

7. The critic for *The Saturday Review* noted that "it is unusual to find the butt in a farce a gentleman, but the innovation is none the less welcome. We do not laugh the less heartily at the little man, and we like him, perforce all the better" (p. 741).

8. *Souvenir Program,* p. 6.

9. *The Times,* p. 10.

10. *Souvenir Program,* p. 21. Brandon Thomas's children, Amy, Silvia, and Jevan had their last names changed to "Brandon-Thomas" after their father's death in 1914. They renewed the copyright on *Charley's Aunt* and held it until it expired on 31 December 1964.

11. Max Beerbohm, *More Theatres* (New York: Toplinger Publishing Co., 1969), pp. 177–78.

12. Anonymous rev. of *The New Boy* by Arthur Law, *The Times,* 22 February 1894, p. 10. (*The New Boy* had an initial run of 428 performances.)

13. Anonymous rev. of *The Strange Adventures of Mrs. Brown* by Robert Buchanan and Charles Marlowe, *The Theatre,* August 1895, p. 107.

14. Anonymous rev. of *The Ladies Idol* by Arthur Law, *The Theatre,* May 1895, p. 300.

15. Anonymous Rev. of *Mrs. Ponderbury's Past* by F. C. Burnand, *The Theatre,* December 1895, p. 346.

16. Anonymous rev. of *The Late Mr. Castello* by Sidney Grundy, *The Theatre,* February 1896, p. 98.

17. Anonymous rev. of *The Jerry Builder* by Mark Melford, *The Times,* 19 June 1894, p. 10.

18. Anonymous rev. of *Mrs. Dexter* by J. H. Darnley, *The Times,* 1 March 1894, p. 7.

19. Anonymous rev. of *The Prodigal Father* by Glen MacDonough, *The Times,* 2 February 1897, p. 10.

20. Anonymous rev. of *The Sunbury Scandal* by Fred Horner, *The Theatre,* July 1896, p. 40.

21. George Bernard Shaw, *The Saturday Review,* 9 May 1896, pp. 473–74.

22. Quoted in *Representative American Drama,* ed. Montrose J. Moses (Boston: Little, Brown and Co., 1941), p. 331.

23. P. M. Augustin Filon, *The English Stage* (London: J. Milne, 1897), p. 284.

24. Walker Stuart, "A Slapstick Renaissance," *The Reporter,* 5 November 1964, p. 40.

25. The first motion picture version was released in 1925 and starred Syd Chaplin as Babbs. The three talking films starred Charles Ruggles (1931), Arthur Askey (1940), and Jack Benny (1942).

26. G. K. Chesterton, "A Defense of Farce," *The Defendant* (London, 1943), p. 95.

Bibliography

The Plays

Albery, James. *The Pink Dominos.* In *The Dramatic Works of James Albery.* Ed. Wyndham Albery. London: Oxford University Press, 1935.

Brough, William and Andrew Halliday. *Going to the Dogs.* London: Thomas Hailes Lacy, 1865.

Byron, Henry James. *Not Such a Fool as He Looks.* In *French's Acting Editions.* Vol. CXX. London, 1868.

——. *Our Boys.* London: Samuel French, 1880.

——. *Uncle.* London: Samuel French, 1883.

——. *The Girls.* In *French's Acting Editions.* Vol. CXXVI. London, 1879.

Buckstone, John Baldwin. *A Dead Shot.* London: The Acting National Drama, 1830.

Burnand, Francis C. *Betsy.* In *French's Acting Editions.* Vol. CXXVIII. London, 1879.

Darnley, J. Herbert. *The Solicitor.* London: Samuel French, 1902.

Darnley, J. Herbert and George Manville Fenn. *The Balloon.* London: Samuel French, 1889.

——. *The Barrister.* London: Samuel French, 1898.

Derrick, Joseph. *Confusion.* In *French's Acting Editions.* Vol. CXXXII. London, 1900.

Gilbert, William S. *Engaged.* London: Samuel French, 1877.

——. *On Bail.* In *French's Acting Editions.* Vol. CXVII. London, 1877.

——. *Tom Cobb, or Fortune's Toy.* London: Samuel French, 1875.

Grundy, Sidney. *The Arabian Nights.* In *French's Acting Editions.* Vol. CXXXIV. London, 1887.

——. *A Pair of Spectacles.* In *Nineteenth Century Plays.* Ed. George Rowell. Oxford: Oxford University Press, 1953.

——. *The Snowball.* In *French's Acting Editions.* Vol. CXXX. London, 1879.

Hawtrey, Charles. *The Private Secretary.* In *French's Acting Editions.* Vol. CXI. London, 1907.

Hay, Frederick. *Our Domestics.* London: Dewitt's Acting Plays, 1868.

Lankester, E. G. *The Gov'nur.* In *French's Acting Editions.* London, 1900.

Melford, Mark. *Turned Up.* London: Samuel French, 1895.

Morton, John Maddison. *Box and Cox.* London: Thomas Haile Lacy, 1847.

——. *Grimshaw, Bagshaw, and Bradshaw.* London: Thomas Haile Lacy, 1851.

Murray, W. H. *Diamond Cut Diamond.* London: Samuel French, 1863.

Pinero, Arthur Wing. *The Cabinet Minister.* Boston: Walter H. Baker, 1893.

——. *Dandy Dick.* Boston: Walter H. Baker, 1893.

——. *The Magistrate.* Boston: Walter H. Baker, 1892.

——. *The Schoolmistress.* Boston: Walter H. Baker, 1892.

Robertson, Tom W. *A Breach of Promise.* In *French's Acting Editions.* Vol. CXXVIII. London, 1869.

Thomas, Brandon. *Charley's Aunt*. London: Heineman Educational Books, 1969.
Thomas, Charles. *The Paper Chase*. London: Samuel French, 1898.
Warren, T. Gideon. *Nita's First*. London: Samuel French, 1888.

Reviews of Late Victorian Farces

Unsigned Reviews

Review of *Aesop's Fables*, by J. P. Hurst. *The Theatre*, July 1889, p. 43.
Review of *Auntie*, by Henry James Byron. *The Theatre*, March 1882, p. 243.
Review of *Betsy*, by Francis Cowley Burnand. *The Theatre*, September 1879, p. 107.
Review of *The Cabinet Minister*, by Arthur Wing Pinero. *The Athenaeum*, 26 April 1890, p. 541.
Review of *The Cabinet Minister*, by Arthur Wing Pinero. *The Saturday Review*, 26 April 1890, p. 501.
Review of *The Cabinet Minister*, by Arthur Wing Pinero. *The Theatre*, May 1890, pp. 312–13.
Review of *Charley's Aunt*, by Brandon Thomas. *The Athenaeum*, 31 December 1892, p. 931.
Review of *Charley's Aunt*, by Brandon Thomas. *The Saturday Review*, 24 December 1892, p. 741.
Review of *Charley's Aunt*, by Brandon Thomas. *The Times*, 22 December 1892, p. 10.
Review of *Comrades*, by Brandon Thomas and B. C. Stephenson. *The Theatre*, February 1883, pp. 108–11.
Review of *Dandy Dick*, by Arthur Wing Pinero. *The Athenaeum*, 5 February 1887, p. 201.
Review of *The Deputy Registrar*, by Ralph Lumley and Horace Sedger. *The Theatre*, January 1889, p. 63.
Review of *Dr. Bill*, by Albert Carré and Hamilton Aidé. *The Theatre*, January 1895, p. 43.
Review of *Girls and Boys*, by Arthur Wing Pinero. *The Times*, 1 November 1882, p. 8.
Review of *The Glass of Fashion*, by Sidney Grundy. *The Saturday Review*, 1 October 1883, p. 202.
Review of *Impudence*, by Arthur Wing Pinero. *The Graphic*, 6 August 1881, p. 261.
Review of *In Chancery*, by Arthur Wing Pinero. *The Saturday Review*, 29 November 1884, p. 619.
Review of *The Ironmaster*, by Arthur Wing Pinero. *The Times*, 18 April 1884, p. 9.
Review of *The Jerry Builder*, by Mark Melford. *The Times*, 19 June 1894, p. 10.
Review of *The Ladies Idol*, by Arthur Law. *The Theatre*, May 1895, p. 300.
Review of *The Late Mr. Castello*, by Sidney Grundy. *The Theatre*, February 1896, p. 98.
Review of *Low Water*, by Arthur Wing Pinero. *Illustrated London News*, 19 January 1884, p. 55.
Review of *The Maelstrom*, by Mark Melford. *The Theatre*, April 1892, p. 207.
Review of *The Magistrate*, by Arthur Wing Pinero. *The Athenaeum*, 28 March 1885, p. 418.
Review of *The Magistrate*, by Arthur Wing Pinero. *The New York Times*, 26 September 1885, p. 5.
Review of *The Magistrate*, by Arthur Wing Pinero. *The Theatre*, April 1885, p. 200.
Review of *The Magistrate*, by Arthur Wing Pinero. *The Times*, 22 March 1885, p. 8.
Review of *The Magistrate*, by Arthur Wing Pinero. *The Saturday Review*, 28 March 1885, pp. 414–15.
Review of *Mrs. Dexter*, by J. H. Darnley. *The Times*, 1 March 1894, p. 7.
Review of *Mrs. Ponderbury's Past*, by F. C. Burnand. *The Theatre*, December 1895, p. 346.
Review of *The New Boy*, by Arthur Law. *The Times*, 22 February 1894, p. 10.
Review of *Nita's First*, by T. Gideon Warren. *The Theatre*, April 1884, p. 218.
Review of *Our Boys*, by H. J. Byron. *Illustrated Sporting and Dramatic News*, 23 January 1875. Rpt. in *Guide to Great Plays*. Ed. Joseph Shipley. New York, 1963.

Review of *Our Boys,* by H. J. Byron. *The Theatre,* October 1878, p. 213.

Review of *The Pink Dominos,* by James Albery. *The Theatre,* April 1877, p. 45.

Review of *The Pink Dominos,* by James Albery. *The Times,* 25 November 1889. Rpt. in *The Dramatic Works of James Albery.* Ed. Wyndham Albery, II, pp. 206-7, London, 1935.

Review of *The Prodigal Father,* by Glen MacDonough. *The Times,* 2 February 1897, p. 10.

Review of *Qwong Hi,* by Fenton MacKay. *The Theatre,* August 1895, p. 111.

Review of *The Rocket,* by Arthur Wing Pinero. *The Athenaeum,* 15 December 1883, p. 786.

Review of *The Rector,* by Arthur Wing Pinero. *Illustrated London News,* 30 April 1883, p. 311.

Review of *The Schoolmistress,* by Arthur Wing Pinero. *The Times,* 29 March 1886, p. 7.

Review of *The Solicitor,* by J. H. Darnley. *The Theatre,* August 1890, p. 86.

Review of *Stop Thief,* by Mark Melford. *The Theatre,* August 1889, p. 305.

Review of *The Strange Adventures of Miss Brown,* by Robert Buchanan and Charles Marlowe. *The Theatre,* August 1895, p. 107.

Review of *The Sunbury Scandal,* by Fred Horner. *The Theatre,* July 1896, p. 40.

Review of *Tom Cobb, or Fortune's Toy,* by W. S. Gilbert. *The Athenaeum,* May 1875, p. 597.

Review of *Turned Up,* by Mark Melford. *The Times,* 18 February 1891, p. 4.

Review of *Turned Up,* by Mark Melford. *The Theatre,* January 1888, p. 84.

Review of *Uncles and Aunts,* by W. Lestoq and Walter Evrard. *The Theatre,* September 1888, p. 153.

Review of *Wanted, A Wife,* by J. H. Darnley. *The Theatre,* July 1890, p. 6.

Review of *A White Elephant. The Theatre,* December 1896, p. 333.

Attributed Reviews

Adams, W. Davenport. Review of *The Gay City,* by George Sims. *The Theatre,* October 1881, p. 237.

Beerbohm, Max. Review of *Dandy Dick,* by Arthur Wing Pinero. *The Saturday Review,* 17 February 1900, p. 63.

Bendall, E. A. Review of *The Member of Slocum,* by George Sims. *The Theatre,* June 1881, p. 364.

_____. Review of *The Mother-in-Law,* by George Sims. *The Theatre,* June 1881, p. 364.

_____. Review of *Themis,* adapted from *Les Pommes de Monsieur Voisin* by Victorien Sardou. *The Theatre,* May 1880, pp. 301-2.

Brandon-Thomas, Amy, Silvia Brandon-Thomas, and Jevan Brandon-Thomas. "Program Notes." *Souvenir Program of Charley's Aunt.* Sixtieth Anniversary Production. Coronation Year 1953.

Clark, H. Saville. Review of *The Pickpocket,* by George Hawtrey. *The Theatre,* June 1886, p. 9.

Howard, Cecil. Review of *The Barrister,* by J. H. Darnley and George Manville Fenn. *The Theatre,* October 1887, p. 214.

Scott, Clement. Review of *The Arabian Nights,* by Sidney Grundy. *The Theatre,* December 1887, pp. 54–63.

_____. Review of *Betsy,* by F. C. Burnand. *The Theatre,* September 1879, p. 107.

_____. Review of *Confusion,* by Joseph Derrick. *The Theatre,* August 1883, p. 109.

_____. Review of *Divorce,* by Robert Reece. *The Theatre,* March 1878, p. 173.

_____. Review of *Engaged,* by William Schwenck Gilbert. *The Theatre,* October 1877, p. 64.

_____. Review of *Flats,* by George Sims. *The Theatre,* September 1881, p. 173.

_____. Review of *The Guv'nor,* by Robert Reece. *The Theatre,* August 1880, pp. 114–16.

_____. Review of *The Magistrate,* by Arthur Wing Pinero. *The Illustrated London News,* 28 March 1885, p. 317.

_____. Review of *Merry Margate,* by Sidney Grundy. *The Theatre,* May 1889, p. 266.

———. Review of *A Pair of Spectacles,* by Sidney Grundy. *The Theatre,* April 1890, p. 108.

———. Review of *The Private Secretary,* by C. H. Hawtrey. *The Theatre,* May 1884, p. 279.

———. Review of *The Schoolmistress,* by Arthur Wing Pinero. *The Theatre,* January 1886, p. 26.

Books and Articles

Adams, J. Q. *The Dramatic Records of Sir Henry Herbert.* New Haven: Yale University Press, 1917.

Albery, Wyndham, ed. *The Dramatic Works of James Albery.* London: Oxford University Press, 1935.

Anonymous, "Our Omnibus Box." *The Theatre,* January 1886, p. 46.

———. "Portraits, VI—Mr. Henry J. Byron." *The Theatre,* October 1878, pp. 212–13.

Archer, William. "Are We Advancing." *About the Theatre.* London: T. F. Unwin, 1886.

———. *English Dramatists of Today.* London: S. Low, Marston, Searle, and Rivington, 1882.

———. *Play-Making.* Boston: Small, Maynard, and Co., 1912.

———. *The Old Drama and the New.* Boston: Small, Maynard, and Co., 1923.

Aristotle. *The Poetics.* Trans. Ingram Bywater. Oxford: Oxford University Press, 1920.

Beerbohm, Max. *More Theatres.* New York: Toplinger Publishing Co., 1969.

Bentley, Eric. *The Life of the Drama.* New York: Athenaeum, 1964.

———. "The Psychology of Farce." *Let's Get a Divorce and Other Plays.* New York: Hill and Wang, 1958, pp. vii-xx.

Bergson, Henri. "Laughter." *Comedy.* Ed. Wylie Sypher. Garden City, New York: Doubleday, 1956.

Bermel, Albert. *Farce: A History from Aristophanes to Woody Allen.* New York: Simon and Schuster, 1982.

Booth, Michael. "Early Victorian Farce—Dionysus Domesticated." *Essays on Nineteenth Century British Theatre.* Ed. Kenneth Richard and Peter Thomson. London: Methuen, 1971, pp. 45–63.

———. *English Plays of the Nineteenth Century: Farces.* Vol. IV. Oxford: Clarendon Press, 1973.

———. *The Magistrate and Other Nineteenth Century Plays.* London: Oxford University Press, 1974.

Chesterton, G. K. "A Defense of Farce." *The Defendant.* London: R. Brimley Johnson, 1943.

Davis, Jessica Milner. *Farce.* London: Methuen, 1978.

Dickinson, Thomas H. *The Contemporary Drama of England.* Boston: Little, Brown, and Co., 1917.

Filon, P. M. Augustin. *The English Stage.* 1898; rpt. London: Benjamin Blom, 1969.

Fowler, H. W. *A Dictionary of Modern English Usage.* Oxford: Oxford University Press, 1965.

Grundy, Sidney. "Dramatic Construction." *The Theatre,* April 1881, pp. 208–11.

Hamilton, Clayton. "Farces and Melodramas." *The Forum,* January 1909, pp. 23–32.

Hawtrey, Charles. *The Truth at Last.* London: T. Butterworth Ltd., 1924.

Hudson, Lynton. *The English Stage 1850*-1950. London: Harrap, 1951.

Hughes, Leo. *A Century of English Farce.* Princeton: Princeton University Press, 1956.

———. "The Early Career of Farce in the Theatrical Vocabulary." *The University of Texas Studies in English,* No. 20 (1940), 82–95.

———, ed. *Ten English Farces.* Austin: The University of Texas Press, 1948.

Hurrell, John Dennis. "A Note on Farce." *Quarterly Journal of Speech,* XLV (1959), 426–30.

Kerr, Walter. *Tragedy and Comedy.* New York: Simon and Schuster, 1967.

Klemm, Werner. *Die Englische Farce im 19 Jahrhundert.* Bern: A. Francke, 1946.

Krutch, Joseph Wood. "The Fundamentals of Farce." *Theatre Arts,* July 1956, pp. 29–30, 92–93.

Maqueen-Pope, W. *Haymarket.* London: Theatre of Perfection, 1948.

Meisel, Martin. *Shaw and the Nineteenth Century Theatre.* Princeton: Princeton University Press, 1963.

Meredith, George. "An Essay on Comedy." *Comedy.* Ed. Wylie Sypher. Garden City, New York: Doubleday, 1956.

Morton, Edward A. "Comedy at the Court." *The Theatre,* September 1887, pp. 142–43.

Nicoll, Allardyce. *The British Drama.* London: Harrap, 1958.

_____. *A History of the English Drama 1660–1900,* 6 vols. Cambridge: Cambridge University Press, 1955–1959.

_____. *A Theory of Drama.* Cambridge: Cambridge University Press, 1931.

Pinero, Arthur Wing. "The Theatre of the Seventies." *The Eighteen-Seventies.* Ed. Harley Granville-Barker. New York: The McMillan Co., 1929.

Pollock, W. H. "A Glance at the Stage." *National Review,* July 1885, p. 646–54.

Scott, Clement. "At the Play." *The Theatre,* September 1879, p. 107.

Simon, Neil. *The Collected Plays of Neil Simon.* New York: Random House, 1979.

_____. Interviewed on *The Dick Cavett Show.* PBS, 14 December 1977.

Stuart, Walker. "A Slapstick Renaissance," *The Reporter.* 5 November 1964, pp. 40–44.

Taylor, John Russell. *The Rise and Fall of the Well-Made Play.* New York: Hill and Wang, 1967.

Wearing, J. P. *The London Stage 1890–99;* A Calendar of Plays and Players. Metuchen, New Jersey: Scarecrow Press, 1976.

Woods, E. P. "Introduction and Notes." *Charley's Aunt* by Brandon Thomas. London: Heineman Educational Books, 1969, pp. vii-xi.

Index

Academy, The, 4

Accents. *See* Diction devices

Actors (*See also* Individual actors), 63, 67–68; as playwrights, 9–10; decline of farce and, 132–33; skill of, and spectacle, 9, 63

Actresses (*See also* Individual actresses), 63

Action: in farce, need for stage management, 21; in French farce, dominance of, 53 —in well-made play, 53–54; disposition of, 50; dominance of, 50; in Act II, 51–52; in Act III, 52–54; pace of, 53–54

Adelphi Theatre, Les dominos roses at, 42

Adolescents, mischievous, in farce, 73

Adultery, subject matter of French farce, 42–43

Afterpiece, farce, 1, 66; British tradition of, 8, 39; characters in, 54–55; demand for, 12, 16–17; eighteenth-century, 8–9; in legitimate theatre, 10–11; in Restoration, 8; nineteenth-century, 12, 14; punning in, 57–58; recurring dialogue in, 34

Aidé, Hamilton, 131

Albery, James (1838–86), 47; adaptations of French farce, 42; Archer on works of, 41; flaws, in works of, 42

Works
—*The Pink Dominos,* 49, 58, 68, 90, 104, adapted, 41–43; influence of, 41, 129, 136; propriety in, 42–43; revival of, *The Times* on, 103; Scott's criticism of, 43; success of, 42; *The Theatre*'s praise of, 43
—*Two Roses,* 41

Allingham, John T., 10

Amazons, The, 124

Archer, William: criticism of farce, 2; on Gilbert's characters, 28; on works of Albery, 41; praise of Pinero's works, 2

Arnold, Samuel, 10

Asides, use in farce, 56–59

Athenaeum, The, 4; on Penley in *Charley's Aunt,* 124; on *Dandy Dick,* 100; praise of *The Magistrate,* 90

Avenue Theatre, The: Burnand's *Mrs. Ponderbury's Past* at, 132; *Dr. Bill* at, 131; revival of *The Private Secretary* at, 131; Shaw's *Arms and the Man* at, 134

Audience, British: eighteenth-century, 8–9; nineteenth-century, 10, 20, 136; Restoration, 8

Bancrofts, The, 22; and Pinero, 79

Beerbohm, Max: on *Charley's Aunt,* 130; on farce, decline of, 130; on *The Magistrate,* 130

Bendall, Ernest A.: on British farce, laughter and, 48; review of *The Member for Slocum,* 48; review of *Themis,* 44; review of *The Mother-in-Law,* 48

Bentley, Eric: on farce, 2, 36; on perception of nineteenth-century playwriting, 2

Bisson, British adaptations of, 44

Blanchard, E.L., praise of British farce, 48

Blue Beard, 132

Booth, Michael, 3

Boucicault, Dion, adaptation of *Forbidden Fruit* (1876), 42

Boucicault, Nina, 132; in *Charley's Aunt,* 120; in Carton's *A White Elephant,* 132

Box sets. *See* Sets, box

Broadhurst, George, *What Happened to Jones* (Strand, 1898), 131

Brough, Fanny: in *The Guv'nor,* 63; in *The Sunbury Scandal,* 133

Bruce, Harry, 68, 70

Buchanan, Robert, *The Strange Adventures of Miss Brown* (Vaudeville, 1895), 130–31; *The Theatre,* on imitation in, 131

Buckstone, John Baldwin, 10, 12, *13;* and Haymarket, 12